Scholarship Search Secrets

From the Perspective of a Student Who Won
Over $700,000 in Scholarships

Pam Andrews

Scholarship Search Secrets: From the Perspective of a Student Who Won Over $700,000 in Scholarships

For information contact:
Pam Andrews
1148 Pulaski Hwy.
Suite 197
Bear, DE 19701

Email : info@TheScholarshipShark.com
Web : www.TheScholarshipShark.com

Cover design by Darrell Andrews, Jr.

First Edition: March 2017

My Challenge To You

Dare to jump into your future with enthusiasm.
Dare to place no limits on what you hope to accomplish.
Dare to dream big and realize it is not just cliché.
Dare to bring excellence to everything you do.
Dare to succeed beyond your wildest expectations.

Introduction

It was the end of the summer before my son entered his senior year of high school. He had just come home from a four-week summer program for high school students at the college where he wanted to earn his BFA in Illustration. He was excited to start apply to his dream school as well as his safety schools – schools where he was confident that would accept him. At the end of the summer, he began writing his admissions essays and gathering recommendation letters. We also began to research scholarships. As we embarked on this journey, we knew that with the rising cost of tuition and our family's value of not accumulating consumer and student loan debt, we knew that we needed to have a plan to pay for college without borrowing massive amounts of loans. As a mother, I did not want my son to start his future with a mountain of debt. But I also did not want money to be the reason why he did not attend his dream school.

Ultimately, I wanted him to know that he could attend college without financial pressures and tremendous debt on himself and our family.

Our plan was to focus on one year at a time by earning just enough scholarships to cover each year. After that, we would establish systems so that he could apply for scholarships each year of undergraduate school.

As we began to work together, I created a system where I would identify scholarships in which he met the eligibility requirements and loaded the information into our scholarship spreadsheet. Each Saturday morning was "Scholarship Saturday," where he would write, edit or re-write essays. Eventually we found a rhythm to this method, and over the course of seven months he had applied to 147 private scholarships. It is from this rigorous process that one Saturday morning my husband described me as a shark when it comes to helping our son apply for scholarships. This is where I got the name, "Scholarship Shark."

For the first few months, he did not win any

scholarships. It was discouraging to work hard and receive notices that you were not a winner. Then in January of his senior year, he received an email stating that he was a semi-finalist for a $10,000 scholarship. We were thrilled! This was the boost that he needed to keep going. Over the next few months, he was notified that he was either a semi-finalist or the finalist for several other scholarships. Eventually, he won eight merit scholarships to individual schools and three other very competitive private scholarships. In all, his scholarship winnings totaled over $700,000. Although our plan had been to take it one year at a time, the Lord supernaturally blessed our efforts so that all four years of college have been paid for through scholarships.

As news about his accomplishment began to spread, I was often asked, "How did you do it? How did he win so much money?" It was from these ongoing conversations with other moms and students like you that this book was written. I wanted to share our strategies and system for winning multiple scholarships.

We could not have done this without a personal relationship with the Lord. It was during those low moments of rejection letters that we both drew on promises found in the Bible that God would truly supply my son's tuition need. My hope is that, as you read this book, you are inspired and encouraged through this journey. It's a tremendous amount of work, but the results make it worth it.

Chapter One
THE COMMITMENT

Winning scholarships takes serious commitment to the process. There are three commitments that you need while going through the process outlined in this book. They are (1) discovering your reason for applying for scholarships, (2) building your team and (3) having the right belief system when it comes to winning scholarships.

Discover Your "Why"

Your reasons for winning scholarships to college should be bigger than you. If the *only* reason you are heading down this path is to avoid student loan debt, then you are missing something bigger. Winning the money should not be the sole focus. The perseverance and resilience that you develop throughout this process will benefit you your entire lifetime. I know that it appears counter-thinking for a book about finding and winning scholarships to state that avoiding student loans should not be your only focus, but when you understand the extra benefits of winning scholarships, then you see that the money is just the cherry on top!

There are many other reasons why it is good to apply for and win scholarships. In a 2008 study by the Association for the Study of Higher Education, it was stated that two main benefits of winning scholarships are that winners go to [their dream] schools and winners are more likely to graduate on time. (Scholarships.com Staff, 2008). In fact, 90 percent of the scholarship winners in this study earned their bachelors degree in four years. This is proving to be a rare accomplishment among students with most students graduating in 6 years.

A 2014 article by the New York Times stated, "The

vast majority of students at American public colleges do not graduate on time, according to a new report from Complete College America, a nonprofit group based in Indianapolis. At most public universities, only 19 percent of full-time students earn a bachelor's degree in four years, the report found. Even at state flagship universities — selective, research-intensive institutions — only 36 percent of full-time students complete their bachelor's degree on time." (Lewin, 2014).

With that in mind, here are a few other benefits of winning scholarships that you may not have considered:

1. Leadership Training – Some scholarship programs provide leadership training for the scholarship recipients. They will pay for the cost of travel to and from the training location, hotel accommodations during the training and meals. In addition to covering

expenses, the scholars receive training at conferences and leadership retreats.

2. Potential internship or job opportunity – If the organization providing the scholarship is related to your career interest, then ask if they offer any internship opportunities or if they know of any other intern opportunities in your field. They will already know that you are a student worthy of winning one of their scholarships so having that honor should give you an advantage when it comes to employment with them.

3. Mentorship and Support – Because the scholarship winners are a reflection of the sponsoring organization, many scholarship programs offer access to mentors, tutors and support to ensure their success on campus. Mentors can help with situations such as finding necessary resources beyond the student's campus, suggesting summer programs which to apply, and filling out

financial aid forms. One more advisor means one more person to support you during your college years.

4. Speaking on behalf of the sponsor – It is not uncommon to be asked to speak on behalf of the sponsoring organization as a scholarship winner. Many donors like to hear from the recipients of scholarships at company and fundraising events. This is a great resume builder and another networking opportunity.

5. Networking with other scholars - National scholarship programs, such as Questbridge National College Match, Prudential Spirit of Community and the GE-Reagan Foundation Scholars, provide opportunities for friendships to form with other scholarship winners. These connections with other students can also lead to learning about other scholarship opportunities or enriching programs.

6. Recognition for your accomplishments --
   Receiving a merit-based scholarship
   indicates that you stand out among your
   peers. It is a way to demonstrate that you
   worked hard and that you have been
   rewarded for your efforts.

There will be days when you do not want to write another essay or apply for another scholarship. Having a few reasons why will help you push through that barrier. Winning scholarships has to be more than just avoiding student loan debt. There needs to be a few other reasons why you want to pursue scholarships. Think of your "why." Why are you applying for scholarships? This commitment to your "why" will anchor you when the process seems long, unrewarding and tiring.

Build Your Team

As a student, you may be feeling overwhelmed with your schoolwork, a part-time job, after school activities, applying to colleges, or preparing for the PSAT, SAT or ACT. Now you feel the extra pressure of not only figuring out what college to attend, but also how to pay for it. On top of this, applying to colleges and applying for scholarships have deadlines that do not care if you have a big exam in your AP Biology class the same day as a deadline for a national scholarship program. While it is important that you feel a sense of urgency during this time, what you do not want is to feel completely overwhelmed, helpless and burned out. After all, these are your high school years and you want to enjoy some, if not most, of your time in high school. This is where your team can step in and help. Your team consists of a parent or mentor, your guidance counselor, recommenders and essay proofreaders. There may be some overlap in the roles. For example, your recommender may also proof read your essays. Your guidance counselor may be your recommender and write a reference letters. Because of this, you can think of the guidance counselor, recommender and essay proofreaders as roles and not necessarily individual. As you are thinking about building your team, think of those who support you during your college planning process.

The first person on your team is a parent or mentor. This is someone who will keep you accountable, help you meet deadlines and give you encouragement along the way. They may also help with finding scholarships, updating your scholarship list, completing applications and mailing them. They will NOT write your essay. This is your responsibility, but they may proofread it and give feedback. This is the person you will rely on the most during your college planning process. Their primary role during this process is to be a support so that you can get maximum results.

The next person you need on your team is your guidance counselor. The guidance office is one of the most underutilized resources in a high school. They can help students with academic advising, college planning, career planning and general counseling on issues such as bullying, drug use, problems at home or any other personal life matter. They will be the individual sending your transcripts and school records for scholarships when requested by the sponsoring organization. Make an appointment to see a school counselor for the first time during freshman year. Try to build a relationship with your guidance counselor throughout the four years of high school. Schedule meetings to discuss your interest, goals, what courses you should be taking, and student activities. The more the school counselor knows about you, the more you can be helped.

Developing the Money Mindset

One often-overlooked step in winning money for college is starting with the right mindset. You will not win money if you have a limiting belief system. A belief is the views and opinions that you have. They are the stories that we tell ourselves that define or shape our thinking. Over time, our beliefs form our belief system. A belief system occurs when our beliefs influence our actions. What we believe is influenced

14

by what we know and with whom we associate. Therefore, it is important to do two things. First, get information about going to college and winning scholarships. Second, find other who do not limit their beliefs in those areas and support you in this endeavor.

When it comes to winning scholarships, believing that only students with high grade point averages, perfect SAT scores, or only students from certain ethnic groups win is an example of a limiting belief system. This thinking will sabotage your efforts. There are scholarships for all types of students, with all kinds of experiences, from all types of backgrounds, and with all kinds of interests.

If you have struggled in the past with believing that you can get into college and win scholarships, then you need to change your thinking. The good thing about a belief is that it can change! To help shape your belief system concerning finding and winning scholarships, this book will provide you with the steps to make this happen. Our method helps you develop a strategy and then a system so that you can have success. The strategy will be what needs to be done and the system will be how to do it. When you begin to see that there is an organized way to go about the scholarship search process, you will begin to see that yes, you can win scholarships to college.

Winning or losing does not start with writing the essay or completing the scholarship application. It starts with your thinking. With you believing that you are capable of winning money. Remember, someone is going to win a scholarship and there is no reason for that someone not to be YOU!

THE SCHOLARSHIP SHARK

Chapter Two
College Financing 101

While this book is primarily focused on winning college scholarships, we must first begin with understanding college financing.

What Will It Cost

It is easy to develop sticker shock at the cost to attend college. This is why it is important to research the true cost of attending college. The true cost of college is not just tuition, but it includes housing, meals, fees, health insurance, student activity fees, technology fees, and health insurance. These are expenses paid directly to the college. Then there are indirect expenses that you are responsible for that are not paid to the university such as transportation, computer and books.

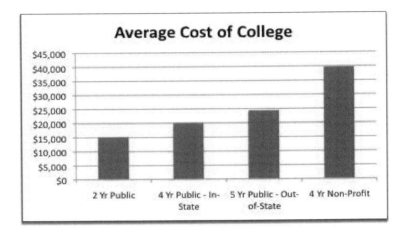

It is important for you to understand the true cost of college so that you have a goal that you are working towards and so that you understand the educational investment that is being made.

Tip: If looking at 4 years of college tuition is too much to handle, try focusing on one year at a time. This makes it manageable, but requires that you commit to the process of winning scholarships throughout your college years. The pro is that it feels more attainable. The con is that each year you will need to go through entire process again, however, because you will be organized to maximize your efforts, it will not be as difficult as the first time.

Terms to Understand

When reading about scholarships and other forms of financial aid, it can be intimidating to hear words and acronyms like EFC, SAR, FAFSA, and COA. I am going to explain all of this to you so that you can start the process armed with one of your greatest tools: knowledge.

FAFSA

FAFSA stands for Free Application for Federal Student Aid. This form is used to determine the amount of money a family is expected to contribute to the price of attending a postsecondary institution. The results of the FAFSA are used in determining student grants, work-study, and loan amounts. In some states, the FAFSA is used to determine the eligibility and amount of state grants.

The FAFSA application is critical because it is used for Federal Pell Grants as well as state grants and other financial aid offered by colleges and universities. You can start completing the FAFSA as early as October 1 the year prior to when you will be attending college. Although the FAFSA information you submit is received by the schools to which you are applying, you do not need to know whether or not you have been accepted to college prior to completing the FAFSA.

The website to complete the FAFSA is https://fafsa.gov/. To get started, you will need a computer and an email address to complete the application. This will allow you to create an FSA ID. It is like your signature on the form, so keep your username and password safe. If you are required to provide parent information on your FAFSA, your parent will create an FSA ID too.

While you are waiting to receive your FSA ID, gather your family's financial information and your information. You will need the following to prepare your FAFSA:

- Your social security number
- If you are a dependent, the social security numbers for one or both of your parents.
- If you or your parents are not U.S. Citizens, your alien registration or permanent resident cards.
- If you worked, your tax returns from two years prior
- If you are a dependent, your parents' tax records from two years prior. For example, if applying for the fall 2018 then you will need 2016 tax returns.

- If your parents live outside of the United States or in Puerto Rico, a copy of your parents' foreign tax return.
- Records of untaxed income in your family such as Social Security benefits, veteran benefits or welfare benefits.
- Bank statements
- Records of investments

If you need help completing the FAFSA, you can call the hotline at 1-800-433-3242.

Two tips for completing the FAFSA

TIP # 1: When completing the FAFSA, fill out the application completely and accurately, and be sure to get it in on time. Even a minor problem with the form could result in delays or the loss of financial assistance.

TIP #2: Even if you think you will not qualify for financial aid because of your income, you should complete it. Actually, there is not an income cutoff to qualify for financial aid. Your eligibility for financial aid is based on a number of factors and not just your income. Also, many states and schools use your FAFSA data to determine your eligibility for your child's aid. Fill out the application and find out what you can get!

SAR

Once your FAFSA is processed, you will immediately receive a Student Aid Report (SAR) with your official Expected Family Contribution (EFC) figure. This report is immediately generated after you complete the FAFSA. Print a copy of your Student Aid Report and file for your records. Within a few days, the schools you listed on your FAFSA will also receive your Student Aid Report. You can request to have your tax information transmitted into the FAFSA application online. This process is quicker and more accurate.

EFC

EFC stands for Expected Family Contribution. It is the amount of money that the federal government expects you to contribute toward the cost of college and it helps determine how much financial aid for which you may qualify. The number is based on the information you submitted while completing the FAFSA.

Here is an example of a Student Aid Report where the Estimated Family Contribution is $7,256.

Example Student Aid Report

Processed Information

Federal Student Aid FAFSA

Form Approved
OMB No. 1845-0001
App. Exp. 12/31/2012

2012-2013 Electronic Student Aid Report (SAR)

The SAR summarizes the information you submitted on your 2012-2013 Free Application for Federal Student Aid (FAFSA).

Application Receipt Date:	01/11/2012	XXX-XX-1234 JO 01
Processed Date:	01/11/2012	EFC: 7256
		DRN: 4557

Comments About Your Information

Based on the information we have on record for you, your EFC is 7256. You may be eligible to receive a Federal Pell Grant and other federal student aid. Your school will use your EFC to determine your financial aid eligibility for federal grants, loans, and work study, and possible funding from your state and school.

WHAT YOU MUST DO NOW (Use the checklist below to make sure that all of your issues are resolved.)

If you have now completed your 2011 tax return, you should correct your information to reflect the income and tax information reported on your tax return. Click 'Make FAFSA Corrections' on the 'My FAFSA' page to make the correction. You may be able to retrieve your tax return information directly from the IRS. If you have not yet completed your tax return, you must correct this SAR to reflect the income and tax information reported on your tax return once it is filed.

If you need to make corrections to your information, click 'Make FAFSA Corrections' on the 'My FAFSA' page. You must use your Federal Student Aid PIN to access your record online. If you need additional help with your SAR, contact your school's financial aid office or the Federal Student Aid Information Center at 1-800-4-FED-AID (1-800-433-3243). If your mailing address or e-mail address changes, you can make the correction online or call 1-800-4-FED-AID and ask a customer service representative to make the change for you.

FAFSA Data

Assumed fields, based on the data you entered, are marked with an '*' (asterisk) sign.

1. Student's Last Name:	JOHNSON
2. Student's First Name:	ANNA
3. Student's Middle Initial:	M
4. Student's Permanent Mailing Address:	123 HOMETOWN STREET
5. Student's Permanent City:	ANYTOWN
6. Student's Permanent State:	MA
7. Student's Permanent ZIP Code:	02115
8. Student's Social Security Number:	XXX-XX-6789
9. Student's Date of Birth:	03/04/1994

COA

COA is Cost of Attendance and is the average cost to attend for a single year. Knowing a college's COA is critical when comparing aid awards. A college with a high COA may offer a generous aid package but still be more expensive than one with a much lower COA. It includes tuition and fees, books and supplies, room and board, transportation, and personal expenses. Colleges adjust the COA yearly to reflect changes to these costs. The college subtracts your Expected Family Contribution (EFC) from the COA to calculate your need for financial aid. The higher the COA, the more aid for which you will be eligible. Because of this, it is sometimes advantageous to attend a higher priced private college than a state school.

How is financial need determined?

Your college first determines whether you have financial need by using this simple formula:

Calculating Your Financial Need

Cost of Attendance (COA)
– Expected Family Contribution (EFC)
= Financial Need

The financial aid office will then send an award letter outlining the amount of financial aid you will receive. The financial aid listed may be a combination of scholarships, grants, work-study and loans. As you win private scholarships, you can reject all or part of the loans and work study listed. Just because it is on your award letter, does not mean that you are obligated to take it.

Calculating the Cost of Attendance

To determine what the university's tuition, boarding and other expenses are, you can either find this information on the college's website or call the admissions office and request to have a catalog with this information sent to you.

Once you have that information, you are ready to begin to calculate what is the cost of attendance. To calculate the cost of attendance in the future, you will do some simple math to adjust for the number of years until your child goes to college.

The following form can be used for each perspective school to determine the cost of attendance.

Calculating the Cost of Attendance

Determine the total tuition cost for the first year

University/College Name:

Cost of tuition:

Cost of housing and meals:

Cost of books:

Cost of fees:

Cost of medical insurance:

TOTAL: $

Now you will determine the future cost of tuition for the first year.

Step 1: What is the number of years until you graduate from high school? _____

Step 2: The answer in Step 1 is the number of times you will multiply the number 1.041. For example, if you graduate in four years, you will multiply 1.041 four times or 1.041 x 1.041 x 1.041 x 1.041 to get the answer of 1.17.

Now, you calculate your answer _____

Step 3: Multiply the number in Step 2 by the total tuition costs. Write that answer below.

Total Cost of Attendance: $

This number tells you approximately what you can expect for your child's first year of college. For the sake of simplicity, this will be the number that we use in all examples. We will not account for the average 4% annual tuition increase each year. Do this calculation for at least three to five schools of interest.

TIP: If you have an unusual circumstance such as unusual medical expenses, tuition expenses, or unemployment, the school's financial aid officer may adjust your Cost of Attendance (COA) or some of the information used to calculate your EFC.

Negotiating The Award Package

You should approach paying for college as you would buying a car: don't even think about paying sticker price. Many colleges don't advertise that they will negotiate aid packages or compete against each other's offers. But many will. The more attractive you are to colleges, the more they are willing to compete, and the more leverage you have.

In some cases, you can ask for more financial aid. Asking for more aid is a process and there are no guarantees. While the school is still determining aid packages, show you have special circumstances that make it impossible to meet the estimated family contribution (EFC). Appeal the initial offer with a letter or an email explaining your circumstance. Special circumstances are financial circumstances that have changed from last year to this year and anything that distinguishes the family from the typical family. Examples include:

- Parent loses a job or experiences a salary reduction.

- The parent's income is volatile, varying a lot from year to year.

- Recent death, disability, incarceration or institutionalization of the student's parent.

- A family member is critically ill.

- The end of child support or Social Security benefits when the child reaches the age of majority.

- The family suffers a financial or natural disaster.

- The student's siblings are enrolled in a private K-12 school.

- There are high dependent-care costs related to a special needs child or elderly grandparent.

- There are high unreimbursed medical and/or dental expenses not covered by insurance.

- Last year's income was affected by one-time events that are not reflective of the family's ability to pay.

- The family is concerned it cannot meet its required contribution

Types of Financial Aid

There are two types of financial aid. They are gift aid and self-help aid.

Gift Aid

Gift aid is money that you do not have to pay back. Naturally, this is the kind of aid that is most desirable. It can take the form of contests, scholarships, grants or cash awards.

1. Scholarships

Scholarships are funds that are used to pay for higher education that do not have to be repaid to the provider. A scholarship is typically awarded based on merit, but also may be awarded based on need or any number of criteria such as ethnicity, a learning disability, a skill, a talent or an unusual attribute. They are available from the federal government, state government, large corporations, small businesses, community organizations, and individual donors. Each scholarship has its own eligibility requirements, award amount, application process and deadline.

2. Grants

Grants are also funds that can be acquired from a variety of sources. Similar to scholarships, they do not need to be repaid. The award amount depends on the level of unmet need and can only be determined after you complete the FAFSA. A grant is usually given only on the basis of need and is determined by the FAFSA.

3. Contests and Cash Awards

Contests are great ways to win money for college. An award given to a student in the form of a check is typically paid directly to the student. Sometimes awards can be tangible items like books, art supplies or computer equipment. Some types of contests are art contests, poetry contests or contests around an issue. A great source for finding contests while in college is the financial aid office, alumni relations, career services and the department chair office. These awards often have fewer applicants and look great on your resume.

Self-help Aid

The most common type of self-help aid is loans. Self-help aid is money that requires a contribution from you. This contribution may mean paying the money back, with or without interest, or working on campus to earn money.

1. Loans

Loans are debt for which you will pay back at a higher amount than you borrow. They can be split into two categories subsidized loans and unsubsidized loans. Subsidized loans are much better than unsubsidized loans because the interest is in deferment, which means that the federal government pays the interest while the student is in college.

Student loans, which are awarded based on need as calculated on your FAFSA, are administered by the college but funded by the federal government. There are also unsubsidized student loans where the interest is not deferred.

2. Work Study

Work-study is financial aid in the form of an on-campus job. Work-study is given in the form of pay for work and is not automatically applied to tuition. It is up to the student to find the job that is paid through the federal work-study program.

Chapter Three

TYPES OF SCHOLARSHIPS

Billions of dollars in financial aid are made available by colleges, businesses, organizations, governmental agencies and private donors each year. Yet, to most people the task of finding financial aid in this vast network of college financing appears to be nearly impossible. When you understand the types of scholarships available, it makes it easier to know how to find them.

Scholarships generally fall in three different categories. They are need-based, merit-based and association-based.   Need-based scholarships are predicated on family income.   There may be a threshold of adjusted gross income that is earned the prior year; it may be determined by your unmet need as calculated on your FAFSA, or some other financial criteria.

Merit-based scholarships are aid awarded on the basis of academics, character, talent, athletic, extracurricular achievement or some other criteria. Merit-based scholarships come from a variety of sources and are typically designed to award performance.

Association-based scholarships are dependent on as many factors as there are associations, businesses and private donors.   The reasons for which scholarships are awarded are vast.

Scholarships have terms or limits on how long you receive the money.   There are one-time scholarships and there are renewable scholarships.   One-time scholarships are awarded one time only, typically for a school year.   This is important because if you earn a one-time award for your first year of college, you will not receive that award automatically in subsequent years.   There are some one-time scholarships that you can apply to each year. If you have won a one-time scholarship, contact the sponsor to see if you are able to reapply each year for that scholarship and what is needed to reapply.

Renewable scholarships are awarded over several years and typically have criteria for maintaining the award such as GPA. The beauty of renewable scholarships is that they have a residual effect. By completing one scholarship application, you have earned money over multiple school years. Contact the funder to see what the eligibility requirements are to renew your scholarship each year. You do not want to lose a scholarship that you worked hard to get.

Strategy: The Layering Technique™

The Layering Technique™ is the method of building two layers of scholarships to meet your financial need. The first layer is earning school merit awards and the second layer is earning private scholarships.

The First Layer

The first place you should look for scholarships is from the universities you plan to attend. Early in the college search process, develop a relationship with the admissions officer. Find out specifically how you can earn a merit award. Some schools call these President or Dean scholarships. This should be your aim at each school to which you apply. Know that many of the merit awards have either early decision or early action deadlines. Early decision is BINDING, meaning that if you are selected for admissions to that school you must withdraw all applications to other schools. With early decision you make a commitment to a particular school and sign a contract. The parent, student, and the school counselor sign this agreement. You should apply to no more than one early decision school and be fairly certain that, if you are admitted, you would want to accept this school.

Early action is not binding and the preferred choice, because you will want to see what each school offers you in his award letter before making a final decision. When applying for early action, you apply to a school and receive a decision early in the process, but you are not legally bound to attend that institution. You may apply to more than one of these options.

Rolling admission is a part of the school's regular admission process. The college reviews the applications as they are received and often awards merit-based aid at the same time. The earlier you apply, the earlier you hear back. Similar to early action, you are not obligated to attend the institution with this option.

Do your homework and inquire with the admissions officer if you are applying for early decision, early action or rolling admission. Applying to colleges early has several advantages. It will let you know if you have been accepted and if so, what merit-based aid is being offered. You will want to confirm that this award is renewable for each year until graduation.

Determining the school's merit awards early in your high school years is recommended. This way, you can plan to meet the requirement over several school years. For example, a school may have a certain score that must be achieved on the SAT or ACT and a minimum GPA requirement to be considered. If you know this your freshman or sophomore year of high school, then you can work toward that goal and make your chances of earning the award greater.

The benefit of earning a merit award from the institution is that they are typically renewable scholarships as long as you maintain a certain GPA. This aid is automatically included in your award letter and there is nothing else that you need to do to ensure that it is credited to your account.

The Second Layer

The second part of The Layering Technique™ is with private scholarships. This is where you find scholarships to fill in the gap between what the school is offering and you need through private scholarships. Private scholarships are third party scholarships and can be applied to any school that you attend. Check with the school's financial aid office to see how third party scholarships impact awards granted to you in the offer letter. Typically, merit awards are not impacted by third party scholarships. However, grants, loans, and work-study may be reduced.

Chapter Four

UNDERSTANDING THE SCHOLARSHIP PROCESS

WHAT DO THEY WANT?

Scholarship committees are not looking for a well-rounded scholar. They are looking for a well-rounded scholarship program. They achieve this goal by selecting individuals are who are passionate about what they do and package that passion. One of the biggest mistakes that students make during their high school years is thinking that more is better. This is not necessarily the case with applying for many merit-based scholarships. Scholarship committees are not interested in a student who has done every extracurricular activity available to him or her. They are interested in students who pursue one or two activities and attained a leadership role in those activities. If your activities are in line with your college major or career goals, then this is even better. The key is to find what you love, be good at it and become a leader in it.

Scholarship committees want a heterogeneous, past winner population. Diversity is not limited to race. There are other areas of diversity considered such as geographic location, first generation college attendees, unique skill or economic diversity.

DON'T GET REJECTED

Nothing can get a scholarship application rejected like misspellings, grammatical errors or leaving parts of the application blank. Another common mistake that students make is not understanding the organization that is awarding the scholarship money. Do a bit of research prior to applying for a private scholarship. If the essay question(s) allow it, weave in the mission of the organization and how being awarded money to attend college ties into that mission. It shows the scholarship committee that you have done your homework.

* * *

Parts of a Scholarship Application

Grades and Test Scores

Although some merit-based awards are earned on stellar essays, there are some that ask for either your GPA or SAT/ACT test scores. This could be the tiebreaker between your well-written essay and another finalist. So, do not neglect your grades during your high school years.

Essays

Completing a scholarship application is all about telling a story. Scholarship committees want to know who you are, what motivates you, what defines who you are and where you are going. It is a way of getting to know the applicants without actually meeting them. A winning essay will either make you stand out or fall flat.

Start by spending a few hours brainstorming about

what to include in the essay. The goal is to make it as memorable as possible. You should think about yourself in relation to the essay question or the sponsoring organization. When writing an essay, make sure to answer all questions on the application. Some essays have multiple parts such as

Describe a time when you lead a group. What was the most challenging part? What did you learn from the experience?

In this example, there are three things that need to appear in the essay. They are (1) talk about leading the group, (2) the challenges and (3) the lessons learned. Missing any of this information may cause the application to get rejected.

As you write essays, you may find that the essay is reusable. If you are submitting an essay previously written for another scholarship, make sure you tailor it to the specific scholarship for which you are applying.

Recommendation Letters

A good reference letter reinforces what other parts of the scholarship application highlight. It should compliment the applicant's credentials and not distract or take away from it. Having a prominent individual such as a business leader or politician write a recommendation letter, unless the recommender personally knows the applicant, is a bad idea. A recommendation letter without specifics about the applicant's credentials can sabotage a great application package. Ask teachers, counselors, or employers who personally know you, your passion and your leadership capabilities for a reference. Typically, you will need no more than two letters. Not all scholarship applications require recommendation letters, however, if it is optional and you have a strong support letter then you will want to include it in your scholarship package.

Interviews

If you are asked to do an interview for a scholarship competition, it means that you are one step closer to winning a scholarship. The interview is an additional opportunity to highlight your personal brand and show their persona. Here are a few things to do to help you do well on a scholarship interview.

1. Prepare in advance

As a serious contender for the award, you will want to prepare. This preparation includes doing a mock interview with a family member or friend. Typical questions are:

> Tell us about yourself?
>
> How have you displayed leadership?
>
> What are your greatest strengths?
>
> What are your greatest weaknesses?
>
> Why should you be awarded this scholarship?
>
> Who are your role models?
>
> Where do you see yourself 5 or 10 years from now?

You should avoid rattling off a laundry list of accomplishments and awards. Instead, use something personal to give the interviewer or panel insight into who you are and why you would be the best choice for the award.

2. Dress to Impress

You need to demonstrate to the scholarship committee that you are a serious student and are honored to have been nominated for the award. First impressions are lasting impressions, so be sure to dress to impress. For boys this means business attire, such as slacks and a button-down, collared white shirt. For girls, this is a knee-length skirt or dress.

3. Arrive Early

Give yourself plenty of extra time to deal with unexpected situations, such as traffic or parking issues, to ensure you do not arrive late. Prior to the interview, write down the name of your interviewer and ask for him/her by name when you arrive.

4. Firm Handshake and Eye Contact

A Fortune 500 CEO once said that when he had to choose between two candidates with similar qualifications, he gave the position to the candidate with the better handshake and eye contact. A handshake and eye contact are not only a form of greeting but are also universal signs of confidence.

5. Send a thank-you note or email

Immediately after the interview, have send either a thank-you email or a thank-you note. Because most final decisions are made immediately after all interviews are completed, I recommend that you send an email over a mailed note.

What about supplemental material?

If possible, reinforce your application with supplemental materials such as newspaper clippings, articles or a resume. I do caution that you not to go too far. If it significantly increases the weight of the application package, then it is probably too much.

Chapter Five

STAND OUT FROM THE CROWD
Develop Your Personal Brand

What is a brand?

A brand is the distinguishing characteristics that make you unique. Your personal brand tells the scholarship committee whether or not you are the right fit and what you will contribute as a winner. Brand is communicated through consistency in application materials. But most important, your personal brand tells them about you. You are in control of your personal brand. You create it. So start thinking about your story, skills, personal experiences and contributions. If you are a freshman or sophomore in high school, then you have time to create the brand you desire. If you are a junior or senior, you will need to think about what your brand is now and how and what you will communicate.

Keep the Message Consistent

You will want to use your essays to showyou're your activities, courses and future goals all work together. Some students try to represent themselves according to their perception of the "ideal applicant" by focusing on the quantity of extra curricular activities and not the quality and consistency of activities. Scholarship committees would rather see passion about one interest than a lack of passion and focus. So try to avoid signing up for every possible activity in high school. In other words, you should find your passion and show how that translates through all you have done.

Consider Your Online Presence

In a 2016 survey with Kaplan Test Prep, college admissions officers, 40 percent say they visit applicants' social media pages to learn about them. In another survey, 67 percent of the schools admitted to Googling a prospective student, and 86 percent admitted to researching students' social media sites. Why? "To protect their school, its reputation, and to avoid potential bad apples from spoiling their brand."

Developing and monitoring your personal brand online is just as vital as what you project on the scholarship application. Do you have social media accounts? What type of pictures do you post on these social media accounts? What are some of your comments? Are they reinforcing or weakening your brand? Remember this information may be viewed by scholarship committees to see who you really are, not just who you say you are.

Make Your Transcript Memorable

1. AP Courses and CLEP Exams

You can make your high school transcript stand out by taking enriching courses outside of your normal course load in your area of interest. You can take courses at your local community college, through your high school with Advance Placement (AP) classes or earn a few college credits by taking and passing the

CLEP (College Level Exam Placement) exam in various subject matters. If you know which school you would like to attend, then contact the office of admissions to see what courses can transfer for college credit. This will give you an added benefit of taking enriching courses. The following links are for CLEP and AP exams:

https://clep.collegeboard.org/
https://apstudent.collegeboard.org/apcourse

2. Outside of School Achievements

Another way to make your transcript sparkle is with academic achievement outside of the classroom. Tournaments, competitions and clubs outside of your school can open the door to more scholarship opportunities. If you have an interest in a particular school subject do research to see if there are competitive opportunities outside of school. Activities such as chess tournaments or STEM competitions are not just limited to the classroom.

3. Volunteering

We all know that volunteering has many benefits

such as connecting us with others and becoming a part of a wide social network of people who share similar interests and passions. But participation in independent projects that further show how you are making a meaningful contribution to your community or the world demonstrate that you not only give of your time and resources, but are passionate about certain issues.

There are two kinds of meaningful volunteering. The first is finding a need or a problem in your community and identifying a way to address it. The second is interest-lead. When it comes to interest-led, what is it that you are passionate about? Is it technology? Is it working with children? Is it caring for the elderly?

4. Summer Pre-College Programs

Spending a summer on a college campus as a high school student in a pre-college program allows students to be immersed in collegiate life. Practically, every college has a pre-college program. Some offer them only to juniors and others at the conclusion of the ninth or tenth grade. The criteria for acceptance also vary from college to college. Pre-college programs allow students to attend classes taught by college professors; live on campus and in most instances earn college credits. Students will have the opportunity to meet people from around the world, exchange experiences, ideas and goals.

You can contact the admissions office of schools that you are interested in or see a list of colleges that offer pre-college programs at http://www.usummer.com/.

Chapter Six

ORGANIZING FOR SUCCESS

There are several tools that you will need to get your scholarship process organized.

Tool #1: Create a new email address

The very first thing you need to do is create a new email account. Most scholarship search engines ask for an email address so that they can send you scholarships listings. Imagine how overloaded a personal email account would be if, along with their other emails, you started receiving those emails. Trust me, it can be a lot of emails to look through each day.

Also, this email address will be where award notices will be received when you win. Because many scholarships have a notification period before moving on to another winner, it is important that you receive notice of winning in a timely manner so that you can respond to the committee. When creating an email name know that this may be the first impression of that the committee has of you and you want it to be a good one. So pick a collegiate sounding or neutral name. Avoid names like 2hot4u@xyz.com or love2party@xyz.com.

You can quickly set up a new email account with any of these free email providers

http://www.google.com

http://www.yahoo.com

http://www.hotmail.com

http://www.outlook.com

http://www.mail.com

Tool #2: Create a calendar

A calendar will become an invaluable tool. Without it, you cannot effectively organize a multitude of scholarships. You can keep a paper calendar and handwrite the scholarship information. However, I prefer an online version so that I get reminders. Calendar services like iCal, Microsoft Outlook or Google Calendar work well for this task. You could also set reminders in your cell phone. Whatever method you choose, the key is not to miss a deadline!

Tip #1: When adding a scholarship to your calendar, never write it on the date it is due. Instead, back up at least two weeks and record it there. For example, if a scholarship has an October 30 deadline, then record it on October 15 instead and make that the target date.

Tip #2: On the calendar, write at least the name of the scholarship, website, due date and dollar amount. This way you will have all of that information in one quick location organized by date.

Tool #3: Use a cloud-based word processor

You will need a way to safely keep copies of all of your essays. Having a cloud-based word processor like Google Docs is a free way to ensure that if your computer crashes, you will not lose those essays. Another reason why I prefer Google Docs is because you can share essays with others to edit for grammar.

Tool #4: Create a supplemental material storage system

A spiral binder or accordion folder will allow you to quickly retrieve anything you may need to include with the scholarship application. Include sections for transcripts, resume, letters of recommendation, SAT/ACT scores, newspaper articles, and scholarships to which you applied. This way when the application asks for something like a reference letter, you already have it and will not waste time asking for one or trying to find one.

Tool #5: Develop a visual measurement for success

It is a rewarding feeling when you visually see progress. There are several reasons why you want to do this. One is to track progress.

My son drew a large thermometer on poster board and displayed it in our kitchen. He wrote what the financial goal for one year was and made incremental markings along the thermometer. It included his faith confession and words of encouragement. You can get very creative with this measurement. Every time my son won a scholarship, he colored in the thermometer. Here are pictures of his thermometer over the course of his senior year when he applied for scholarships.

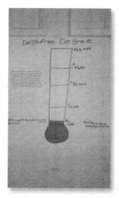
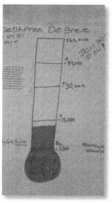

Chapter Seven

SEARCHING FOR SCHOLARSHIPS

Now, we are at the fun part: searching for scholarships! As you search, you will find that there are many scholarships and many places to search. Our approach to finding scholarships consists of three steps. First, create a list of all scholarships where you meet the eligibility requirements. Second, prioritize by the deadline (remember to change this date to two weeks prior.) Third, apply to every scholarship – large or small- where the requirements match your eligibility. By following this three-step approach, you will have a massive list of scholarships that closely match your achievements and background.

Websites

The Internet has streamlined the search process and makes it easier than ever to find scholarships and grant opportunities to help students cover the costs of higher education. Specialized websites allow you to just answer a few questions and find hundreds of potential sources for scholarships. You can begin with a scholarship search website where you can find many scholarships, from those based on your intended major or your hobbies, and even unusual scholarships, in a relatively short amount of time. Because there are so many free scholarship search engines available to students online, it can be difficult to know which websites to use. The best websites will update their database often, keep their information private, and select scholarships that are a good match. With these criteria in mind, I suggest the following scholarship websites:

www.fastweb.com
www.scholarships.com
www.goodcall.com

www.salliemae.com/scholarships

www.collegeboard.com

www.collegenet.com

www.moolahspot.com

I recommend setting up profiles on multiple sites so you catch as many opportunities as possible. Remember to have a separate email address dedicated to the scholarship search process. You will be surprised at the quantity of emails you will receive with scholarship opportunities.

Scholarship Directories

Prior to the Internet, the most common way to search for scholarships was by thumbing through the pages of enormous scholarship directories. Although this can be time consuming, it is still a good place to search because not all scholarships are listed on scholarship websites. You can purchase these books or borrow them from the public library. A few of our favorite books are the Scholarship Handbook by The College Board, Scholarships, Grants & Prizes by Peterson's, and any financial aid book written by Gail A. Schlachter. She has published a series of scholarship directories for specific groups such as Financial Aid for Women, Financial Aid for African Americans and Financial Aid for Hispanic Americans. When searching, do not start at the front of the book and leaf through; this will take too much time. Instead, use the index in the back of the book to find the scholarships you want.

High School Guidance Counselor

The guidance office receives scholarship notices for local, regional and national scholarships. Ask your guidance counselor if they have a list of scholarships. They may post them on a bulletin board, the school's website, or have them filed away in a cabinet. The key is that you should take the initiative by approaching them and not wait for the guidance counselor to contact you.

High School Websites

Do not be limited to the school you attend. Although you may not be able to approach the guidance counselor at another school, that does not mean that you may not be able to get scholarship information. Check to see if area high schools post scholarship opportunities on their website. If there is a search box on the school's website, then type the word "scholarship" in the box to see what you find. You can do this with schools in other districts also.

College Websites

Not only is your prospective college a great place to search, but other colleges may list scholarships on their websites as well. Talk with the financial aid officer at your prospective school and let them know that you are interested in applying to third party, private scholarships.

Student Clubs

If you participate in any high school or after-school clubs, you may be eligible for scholarships. Start by talking with the club's leader to let them know that you are interested in applying to scholarships. Often club-sponsored scholarships require the nomination of the advisor or someone within the organization.

Civic Organizations

Community organizations such as Elks, Jaycees, Kiwanis, Lions and Mason/Eastern Stars often have funds designated for local college-bound students. Some require a nomination or reference from a member. Most of these scholarships are offered on the local level and typically have fewer applicants. Call around to groups in your area to see what scholarships they offer.

Sororities and Fraternities

Fraternities and sororities are a good place to look for scholarships. National sororities and fraternities usually feature a separate foundational branch that raises funds that seek endowments to establish scholarships and grants. To find a complete list of sororities and fraternities, visit:

Sorority
http://www.greekrank.com/sororities/
Fraternity
http://nicindy.org/about/members/

Employers

Check with employers to see if they offer scholarships to the children or grandchildren of employees. Many large companies have grants and scholarships that are not publicized to the general public. The company's human resources officer would be the best point of contact.

Advocacy Organizations for Ethnic Groups

There are a myriad of ethnic group associations. Below is a list of just a few examples of advocacy groups that offer scholarships by ethnic groups:

African-American
- NAACP www.naacp.org
- United Negro College Fund www.uncf.org

Asian Pacific Americans
- OCA – Asian Pacific American Advocates http://www.ocanational.org
- Ascend Pan-Asian Leaders http://www.ascendleadership.org

Hispanic
- National Hispanic Scholarship Fund http://www.hsf.net

Italian-Americans

- National Italian American Foundation
  http://www.niaf.org

Native American
- Bureau of Indian Affairs
  http://www.doi.gov/gureau-indian-affairs.html
- Native American Scholarship Fund
  http://www.ihs.gov

Religious Groups

The Presbyterian Church in the USA, United Methodist Church, and Aid Association for Lutherans are among the group of religious organizations with national scholarships. Many local churches also sponsor scholarship programs for members and/or students in their community. Some Christian colleges will match a church's scholarship to a student.

Military Groups

There are scholarship programs that target children of military personnel whose parents may be active duty members of the armed forces, war veterans, deceased, disabled, MIAs and former POWs.

Chapter Eight

WHAT TO DO IF YOU DO NOT WIN

You have waited for a decision for months and now you open an email with the subject: Scholars Program Notification. You read the following:

Thank you for taking the time and effort to apply to the Scholars Program. We regret to inform you that you were not selected as a recipient. Many excellent students applied and the program was extremely competitive this year. In a competitive scholarship program, not every student can receive an award.

Receiving this news after you have done so much work can be frustrating, but you cannot quit. You must keep applying for scholarships. It can be disappointing to put the work in and not receive any money. However, you are never going to win a scholarship unless you apply. Also, there is so much to be learned from the scholarship that you did not win.

The first thing you should do is take a look at why you did not receive the award. Sometimes rejection letters give clues as to the type of students they desired. Second, take a look at the application submitted. Were you missing documents? Did the application get rejected because it was not completed thoroughly? Did you miss a deadline? If any of these are the reasons, then those are easy mistakes to correct for future applications.

What if all of those things were done correctly? Maybe it was the essay or the personal statement. Was the essay or personal statement well written? How can it be improved? Ask your guidance counselor or a friend what could have been done to make it better. If you are able, contact the sponsor to get a list of the winners. Some organizations will give you copies of winning essays or publish them on their website. Use this information to improve your chances on the next essay you write.

Sometimes it is none of those reasons. Sponsors may be looking for a specific type of candidate and maybe you simply did not match their profile although you were eligible to apply. For example, my son was a semi-finalist for a large, competitive scholarship. There were over 13,000 students who applied. He received a notice that he was one of 100 selected as a semi-finalist and they needed more information. After submitting his leadership information, he did not win as one of the 20 finalists. When we read the profiles of the twenty students selected, all of them had civic-related leadership skills, where my son had more community-based leadership skills.

If you are able to apply the following year to a scholarship that you did not win, by all means do so. Do not assume that you are only eligible to apply once unless it is specified in the eligibility requirements. You may actually win the second time around.

In closing, a rejection letter does not mean that you are not good enough. It may mean that you may not be a good fit for the sponsor's organization or that you to improve what was submitted. The key is to keep applying to as many scholarships as your eligibility will allow.

Chapter Nine

WHAT TO DO IF YOU WIN

Imagine that in your hand is a letter addressed from one of the scholarships to which you applied. You have waited for this notification for quite a while. After opening it, you read the following:

> *On behalf of the ABC Foundation it is my great pleasure to inform you that you have been selected as the recipient of the Leadership Scholarship, worth $1,000. This is truly an outstanding accomplishment. The Scholarship Committee felt that your application was quite strong. Congratulations!*

Opening a letter like that makes all of the hard work worth it. It gives you the fuel to keep going to reach your goals. Celebrate this success! After you win, there are a few other things that you should do.

Say "Thank You"

Send a thank you letter to the sponsoring organization thanking them for their generosity and financial support. After talking with one foundation, I discovered that few winners take the time to write a thank you note. You will want to continue to stand out as an applicant by showing their gratitude.

Thank anyone who helped you with the process. This would be the recommender or the person who wrote a reference letter. Also thank anyone who proofread your essays or applications.

Follow Through With the Award

Complete paperwork in a timely manner so that the sponsor can process your award. You may need your school's address to send directly to the school.

Contact the financial aid officer notifying them that you have won and determine how this impacts existing aid granted by the school, if at all. If you exceed the cost of attendance, you may be able to get a refund. This is typically called "overpayment" and is refunded to the student. Yes, this can happen where you receive more scholarships and grants than the cost of attendance. Save this money for future educational expenses that you may have to pay out of pocket such as books, if the scholarship allows.

Monitor and confirm that all the funds are credited to your tuition bill. Failing to stay on top of this one area can cost your family thousands of dollars without ever knowing. Because mistakes can be made, it is important for you to be on top of financial aid, especially when awarded scholarships outside of the school.

Press Releases

Send out a press release to your local newspaper. Some scholarships will have a standard press release that you can send that will mention their organization and the work that they do. Remember to add personal information about yourself, such as your major and future career goals.

Update Scholarship List

Update your progress chart and/or scholarship

spreadsheet. You will want to keep a visual reminder of where you are so that you can continue to work towards your scholarship goals.

Chapter Ten

CONCLUSION

Note to Parents

Moms and Dads, you play an incredibly important role during this stage of your child's life. Applying for scholarships can be emotionally draining and overwhelming. One of the greatest roles you can have during this time is one of encourager, supporter and listener. Be prepared to allow your child to vent about the process. Sometimes all your child needs is a reminder of the benefits and that it will be worth all of the work. Other times they may need to take a break from all of it. During those moments, allow them to pause and pick it up again in a few weeks. Each parent-teen relationship is different, so do what works best for you.

Note to Students

In closing, I want you to know that you can do this! It takes work, but it is worth it. The key is to develop a plan and stick with it. Make the commitment to the process and work your plan.

LIST OF SCHOLARSHIPS

SCHOLARSHIPS BY MONTH
JANUARY

John F. Kennedy Profiles in Courage Essay Contest
Eligibility: The contest is open to United States high school students in grades nine through twelve attending public, private, parochial, or home schools; U.S. students under the age of twenty enrolled in a high school correspondence/GED program in any of the fifty states, the District of Columbia, or the U.S. territories; and U.S. citizens attending schools overseas.
Deadline: January 4
Awards: Multiple awards ranging from $100 to $20,000
Website:
https://www.jfklibrary.org/Education/Profile-in-Courage-Essay-Contest.aspx

Ronald Brown Scholars Program
Eligibility: Black/African American, must be a rising high school junior or senior. Have a strong academic record, demonstrated leadership and active involvement at school and/or in the

community.
Deadline: January 9
Award: $40,000 ($10,000/year)
Website: http://www.ronbrown.org

Prompt Essay Contest
Eligibility: For high school seniors, use any essay you've written.
Deadline: January 15
Awards: Multiple awards ranging from $2,000 to $20,000
Website: https://www.prompt.com/scholarship/

GE-Reagan Foundation Scholarship
Eligibility: Demonstrated leadership, drive, integrity, and citizenship; minimum 3.0 grade point average, citizens of the United States of America; high school seniors attending high school in the United States (students living on U.S. Armed Forces base and homeschooled students are also eligible)
Deadline: January 5
Award: $40,000 ($10,000/year)
Website: http://www.reaganfoundation.org/GE-RFScholarships.aspx

Mensa Foundation
Eligibility: Applicants must intend to enroll in an accredited educational institution for the upcoming school year.
Deadline: January 15
Award: $500 to $1,000
Website:

http://www.mensafoundation.org/what-we-do/scholarships/us-scholarship-process/

Asian & Pacific Islander American Scholarship Fund (APIASF)

Eligibility: Asian American and Pacific Islander (AAPI) high school and college students who will be enrolling or are currently enrolled in a U.S. accredited college or university as a degree-seeking undergraduate student in the upcoming academic year.
Deadline: January 11
Awards: $2,500 to $20,000
Website: http://www.apiasf.org

Free Speech Essay

Eligibility: High school juniors and seniors who are U.S. citizens or permanent residents must submit an essay between 800 and 1,000 words on the provided topic.
Deadline: January 1
Awards: $500 to $10,000
Website: https://www.thefire.org/student-network/essay-contest/#prompt

FEBRUARY

Jackie Robinson Foundation

Eligibility: Minority high school students with demonstrated leadership and community service, SAT score of 1,000 on math and critical reading or a composite ACT score of 21.

Deadline: January 11
Awards: $28,000 (over 4 years)
Website: http://www.jackierobinson.org

The Vegetarian Resource Group
Eligibility: High school students who have promoted vegetarianism in their schools and/or communities.
Deadline: February 20
Awards: $5,000 t0 $10,000
Website:
http://www.vrg.org/student/scholar.htm

Herff Jones Believe in U Scholarship
Eligibility: High school students
Deadline: February 28
Awards: $2,000
Website:
https://www.herffjones.com/biuscholarship/

Alzheimer's Foundation of America
Eligibility: Plan to enter an accredited college/university within 12 months of the scholarship deadline. Be currently enrolled in a public, independent, parochial, military, home-school or other high school in the United States.
Deadline: February 15
Awards: $500 to $5,000
Website:
http://www.youngleadersofafa.org/about_new.ht
ml

Church's Scholars Program

Eligibility: High school seniors
Deadline: Mid-February
Award: $1,000
Website:
http://www.churchs.com/neighborhood.php

Future Farmers of America
Eligibility: Scholarships for members of FFA and
some available to non-FFA meeting sponsor
criteria.
Deadline: February 1
Award: $1,000
Website: https://www.ffa.org/scholarships

MARCH

Engebretson Foundation Scholarship
Eligibility: High school senior with a composite
or higher on the ACT exam (or at least 1240 on
the SAT), have achieved at least a 3.75 GPA or
above and/or top 5% of graduating class.
Deadline: March 1
Award: $5,000/semester
Website:
http://www.engebretsonfoundation.org/

Women Western Golf Foundation Scholarship
Eligibility: High school senior girls who intend to
graduate in the year of application. Must be U.S.
citizens and meet entrance requirements of and
plan to enroll at an accredited four-year college or
university.

Deadline: March 1
Award: $8,000 ($2,000/year)
Website:
http://wwga.org/WWGA.org/Scholarship_Inform
ation.html

German Russian Heritage Society Adult Essay
Contest
Eligibility: Contest is open to all adults, both
members and non-members of GRHS. Contestant
must submit an essay on a topic elated to
German Russian history, heritage or culture.
Contestant does not need to be ethnic German-
Russian to enter contest.
Deadline: March 1
Amount: $500
Website:
http://www.grhs.org/youthn/current/current.ht
ml

Bob Warnicke Scholarship
Eligibility: Applicants must be a high school
senior planning to attend a four year university
and an active member of National Bicycle League.
Deadline: March 1
Award: $500 to $5,000
Website:
http://www.usabmx.com/site/postings/819

Barbara Wiedner and Dorothy Vandercook Peace
Scholarship
Eligibility: Applicant must be a high school senior
or college freshman who can provide evidence of

leadership and/or personal initiative in activities or in an organization relating to peace and social justice, nuclear disarmament, and/or conflict resolution.
Deadline: March 1
Amount: Up to $500
Website: http://peacescholarships.org/

1000 Dreams Scholarship
Eligibility: Scholarship is open to high school and college women who can demonstrate financial need. Applicant will need to submit a completed application and at least one letter of recommendation.
Deadline: August and March
Award: Up to $1,000
Website: https://www.growyourgiving.org/scholarships/1000-dreams-scholarship-fund

Blacks at Microsoft Scholarships
Eligibility: Scholarship is open to high school seniors of African descent who plan to attend a four-year college or university in the fall. Must have at least a 3.3 GPA. Applicant must be pursuing a bachelor's degree in engineering, computer science, computer information systems or select business programs.
Deadline: March 1
Amount: $5,000/year up to $20,000 total
Website: https://www.microsoft.com/en-us/diversity/programs/blacks-scholarships.aspx

Children of Warriors National Presidents' Scholarship
Eligibility: Scholarship is open to daughters, sons, grandsons, granddaughters, great-granddaughters, great-grandsons or veterans who served in the Armed Forces during WWI, WWII, Korean War, Vietnam War, Lebanon and Grenada, Panama, or Desert Shield/Storm Gulf/War on Terrorism.
Deadline: March 1
Amount: Up to $3,500
Website:
https://www.alaforveterans.org/scholarships/children-of-warriors-national-presidents--scholarship/

Beyond the Boroughs Scholarship
Eligibility: High school seniors with 2.5 GPA or higher, involvement in extra-curricular activities and low household income
Deadline: March 15
Amount: Up to $20,000 over 4 years
Website: http://www.beyondtheboroughs.org

Life Lessons Essay Contest
Eligibility: Scholarship is open to legal residents of the 50 United States, the District of Columbia and Puerto Rico, who are between 17 and 24 years of age and have experienced the death of a parent or legal guardian. Applicant must be currently enrolled in, or have been accepted to, a college, university or trade school.
Deadline: March 1

Amount: $5,000 to $15,000
Website: http://www.lifehappens.org/life-lessons-scholarship-program/

Davidson Rubber Division Scholarship
Eligibility: Scholarships is open to junior and senior students who are majoring in chemistry, physics, chemical engineering, mechanical engineering, polymer science or a rubber industry-related field.
Deadline: March 1
Amount: $5,000
Website: http://www.rubber.org/student-scholarships

APRIL

Business Plan Scholarship for Students with Disabilities
Eligibility: Scholarship is open to students enrolled in an undergraduate or grade degree program at any accredited American College, University or Trade School with a documented disability.
Deadline: April 15
Award: $1,000
Website: http://fitsmallbusiness.com/learn-how-to-write-a-business-plan/

Champions for Christ
Eligibility: Scholarship is open to students who have surrendered their lives to full-time Christian service and are preparing for full-time Christian

ministry.
Deadline: April 26
Award: $500 to $1000
Website:
http://www.championsforchrist.us/~cfc/awards
/

Visionary Scholarship Program
Eligibility: Scholarship is open to high school
freshmen, sophomore, junior, or senior students
who are United States citizens or eligible non-
citizens. Applicant must submit an essay on why
college is important to them.
Deadline: April 1
Award: Up to $5,000
Website:
http://www.americancollegefoundation.org

Wergle Flomp Humor Poetry Contest
Eligibility: Contest is open to poets of all ages and
from all nations. Contestant must submit one
English poem only, with a maximum of 250 lines.
Deadline: April 1
Award: Up to $1,000
Website: https://winningwriters.com/our-
contests/wergle-flomp-humor-poetry-contest-free

The Herbert Lehman Education Fund
Scholarship
Eligibility: Graduating senior, first year student
or transfer student with a commitment to public
service.
Deadline: April 1

Award: Up to $8,000 ($2,000/year)
Website: http://www.naacpldf.org/herbert-lehman-education-fund-scholarship

FISCA Scholarship
Eligibility: For outstanding college bound high school senior, from each of the five geographic regions across the nation. Two scholarships for each region are given.
Deadline: April 8th
Award: $2,000
Website:
http://www.fisca.org/content/navigationmenu/community/outreach/fiscanationalscholarshipprogram/default.htm

SRSI Foundation Scholarship
Eligibility: Scholarship is open to U.S. citizens enrolled in a four-year bachelor degree program in Civil Engineering, Civil Engineering Technology, Construction Engineering, Construction Technology, Construction Management, Construction Information Technology, or Architectural Engineering.
Deadline: April 4
Award: $1,500
Website: http://crsi-foundation.org/index.cfm/scholarships/programs

Denena Points, P.C. Law and Technology Scholarship
Eligibility: Scholarship is open to current high

school and college students with a 3.0 or higher GPA. Applicant must submit an essay on how technology can make law more accessible.
Deadline: April 15
Award: $1,000
Website: http://www.denenapoints.com/scholarship/

Barron Prize for Young Heroes
Eligibility: Prize is open to students between the ages of 8 and 18 years of age who are permanent residents of the United States or Canada. Applicant must be nominated for an extraordinary service activity which has clearly benefited other people or the planet we share.
Deadline: April 15
Award: $5,000
Website: http://barronprize.org/apply/

Mattress Clarity Scholarship Program
Eligibility: Scholarship is open to graduating high school seniors and current college students. Applicant must create a video sharing personal information about their education and goals.
Deadline: April 30
Award: $1,000
Website: https://www.mattressclarity.com/scholarship-program/

MAY

Community Involvement Scholarship

Eligibility: Scholarship is open to students entering their first year of college at the beginning of the fall. Applicant must be deeply involved in the community that surrounds them through direct involvement, meaningful commitment and generosity of their time and efforts.
Deadline: May 1
Award: $1,000
Website: http://www.indianapilaw.com/hs-community-award/

Directron.com
Eligibility: Applicants must submit an essay with a topic that is related to computer technology.
Deadline: May 1
Award: $500
Website: www.directron.com/scholarship.html

Seth Okin Good Deeds Scholarship
Eligibility: Scholarship is open to any student pursing a post-secondary education who is both interested and engaged in serving their community.
Deadline: May 1
Award: $500
Website: http://criminallawyermaryland.net/

Mike Reynolds Scholarship
Eligibility: Scholarship is open to students who will be sophomores, juniors, or seniors at the time the scholarship is awarded and is pursuing careers in radio, television, or digital journalism.
Deadline: May 31

Award: $1,000
Website:
http://www.rtdna.org/content/mike_reynolds_jo
urnalism_scholarship

Steve Duckett Conservation Scholarship and
Essay Contest
Eligibility: Scholarship is open to current college
students in good academic standing who can
demonstrate a commitment to environmental
conservation using past and present volunteer,
professional, and education experiences.
Deadline: May 1
Award: $500
Website: http://www.virginiacriminallaws.com

Brower Youth Awards
Eligibility: Recognizes six people ages 13 to 22
living in North America who have shown
outstanding leadership on a project or campaign
with positive environmental and social impact.
Deadline: May 15
Award: $3,000 cash prize, a professionally
produced short film about their work from an
Emmy award winning film crew, and flight and
lodging accommodations for a week long trip to
the San Francisco Bay Area.
Website: www.broweryouthawards.org

My Projector Lamps Scholarship
Eligibility: Scholarship is open to graduating high
school seniors and current college students who
are at least 16 years of age. Applicant must

submit an essay on a given topic related to the use of multimedia and data visualization in K-12 classrooms.
Deadline: May 1
Award: $500
Website:
http://www.myprojectorlamps.com/scholarships.html

Rentacomputer Cares Scholarship
Eligibility: Scholarship is open to high school students who will be attending college within the next 12 months and current students working towards a degree. Applicant must submit a 500-word essay describing their academic and career goals.
Deadline: May 31
Award: $500
Website:
https://www.rentacomputer.com/cares/scholarships

JUNE

Aspiring Animation Professional Scholarship
Eligibility: Scholarship is open to graduating high school seniors who intend to purse an animation related field at an accredited post-secondary school or college.
Deadline: June 1
Award: $1,000
Website:
http://www.animationcareerreview.com/animati

oncareerreviewcom-aspiring-animation-
professional-scholarship-program

Jack & Jill Foundation Scholarships
Eligibility: African American/Black high school
seniors with a 3.0 or higher GPA. Cannot be a
member of Jack & Jill.
Deadline: June 1
Award: $1,500 to $2,000
Website:
http://jackandjillfoundation.org/scholarships/

Automotive Hall of Fame
Eligibility: High school senior with a 3.0 GPA or
higher and an interest in the automotive
industry.
Deadline: June 30
Award: Varies
Website:
http://www.automotivehalloffame.org/education

Adam Greenman American Dream Scholarship
Eligibility: Currently enrolled in college or a high
school senior. Must have a minimum of 3.25
GPA. Preference is given to naturalized or first-
generation American citizens.
Deadline: June 1
Award: $1,000
Website:
http://www.adamgreenmanlaw.com/diversity-
scholarship/

CFA Institute September 11 Memorial

Scholarship
Eligibility: Scholarship is open to students who were dependent children, spouses or domestic partners on September 11, 2001 of those person who died or were permanently disabled as a direct result of the September 11th attacks. Applicant must be planning to enroll or already enrolled in part-time or full-time undergraduate study at an accredited two- or four-year college or university and studying finance, economics, accounting, or business ethics.
Deadline: June 15
Award: Up to $25,000
Website:
http://www.sms.scholarshipamerica.org/cfainstitute/

Athnet Sports Recruiting Scholarship
Eligibility: Scholarship is open high school seniors or current college students who are current or former high school or college athletes. Applicant must submit an essay on the lessons they have learned playing sports.
Deadline: June 1
Award: $1,000
Website:
http://www.athleticscholarships.net/scholarship-contest.htm

Blue Fire Broadband Rural Scholarship Essay Contest
Eligibility: Scholarship is open to graduating high school seniors and current students with a 2.5

GPA or higher who will be enrolled at an accredited college or university. Applicant must submit an essay on a given topic related to rural areas.
Deadline: June 1
Award: $500
Website:
http://www.bluefirebroadband.com/scholarship

Helen Gee Chin Scholarship Foundation
Eligibility: Scholarship is open to U.S. citizens who plan to or are currently enrolled full-time as an undergraduate at an accredited U.S. four-year college or university for the entire academic year. Applicant must have studied one or more of the Chinese Martial Arts – Kung Fu, Wu Shu, or Tai Chi – for a minimum of five years.
Deadline: June 15
Award: $2,500
Website:
http://www.hgcscholarshipfoundation.org/home/eligibility

Aftermath Services Scholarship
Eligibility: Scholarship is open to students currently enrolled in an institution of higher education, or graduating high school seniors enrolling in the fall. Applicant must submit an essay on a given topic related to social media.
Deadline: June 30
Award: $1,000
Website:
http://www.aftermath.com/scholarship/

Dell Corporate Scholars Program
Eligibility: Minority students enrolled full-time at a U.S. located accredited four-year who are juniors at the time of the application. Applicant must major or have an academic focus in Supply Chain Management, Engineering, Electrical Engineering, Computer Science, or Information Technology.
Deadline: June 30
Award: Up to $4,500
Website:
https://scholarships.uncf.org/Program/Details/02f84698-99c8-4d40-ab83-1ec4ef9a5a76

Discountrue Scholarship
Eligibility: Scholarship is open to incoming and current college students. Applicant must submit an essay on a given topic related to taking care of the planet.
Deadline: June 30
Award: $3,000
Website:
https://www.discountrue.com/scholarship

JULY

AFIO Scholarship
Eligibility: Undergraduate scholarships, applicants must be entering their junior, or senior year by the summer. For Graduate scholarships, applications must be submitted no earlier than your senior undergraduate year and no later than your second year of graduate

studies.
Deadline: July 1
Award: From $1,000 to $3,500
Website:
https://www.afio.com/13_scholarships.htm

Axol Science Scholarship
Eligibility: Scholarship is open to students
enrolled or accepted for a graduate or
undergraduate degree for the 2016/2017
academic year. Applicant must be pursuing a
degree program/research area in a life science
related field. Applicant must submit an essay on
a topical life-science subject.
Deadline: July 1
Award: $2,000
Website: https://www.axolbio.com/page/axol-
science-scholarship

Ashley Soule Conroy Foundation Scholarship
Eligibility: Scholarship is open to students
currently enrolled as an undergraduate student
at a four-year college or university in the United
States and are planning to participate in full-time
study abroad for at least one full semester
outside of the United States.
Deadline: July 1 and December 1
Award: $3,000
Website: http://www.ashleysfoundation.org/

From Failure to Promise Scholarship
Eligibility: Contest is open to high school
seniors, undergraduate, and graduate-level

college students with at least a 2.5 GPA.
Applicant must answer three given prompts
related to the book, "From Failure to Promise:
360 Degrees."
Deadline: July 31
Award: Up to $10,000
Website:
http://www.fromfailuretopromise.com/essay-
scholarship-contest--html

BooKoo Scholarship
Eligibility: Scholarship is open to graduating
high school seniors and current college students
attending an accredited college or university.
Applicant must submit an application and
answer questions related to the applicant's
educational plans.
Deadline: July 1 and December 1
Award: $1,000
Website: http://www.bookoo.com/scholarships

IP Video Contest
Eligibility: Contest is open to individuals 13
years of age or older. Contestants between the
ages of 13 and 18 must be enrolled as a full-time
student in an accredited secondary, college level
or trade school. Contestant must create a video
answering one of the given questions related to
the patent system.
Deadline: July 1
Award: Up to $5,000
Website: http://www.ipvideocontest.com/

Atlanta Dental Spa Scholarship
Eligibility: Scholarship is open to students who
will be attending college in Fall 2016. Applicant
must submit a short video sharing what they will
do in life to make people smile.
Deadline: July 31
Award: $1,000
Website:
http://atlantadentalspa.com/scholarship.html

Signal Grace Scholarship Contest
Eligibility: Scholarship is open to high school and
college students in the United States. Applicant
must read the memoir Signal Grace and create
an entry in response to one of three given
prompts.
Deadline: July 4
Award: $1,000
Website: http://tmyates.com/win-money-for-
school/

Korean American Scholarship
Eligibility: Scholarship is open to
undergraduates, graduates, and graduating high
school seniors who have Korean heritage and are
studying in the United States regardless of
citizenship (including Korean Nationals).
Deadline: July 8
Award: Up to $5,000
Website: http://www.kasf.org/application#

Resume Companion LLC
Eligibility: Applicant must be enrolled, or due to

be enrolled in full-time university education for the semester they are applying to receive the scholarship. Applicant must create a resume based on the life of any fictional or non-fictional character, from TV, history, literature or myth.
Deadline: July 14
Award: $1,000
Website:
https://resumecompanion.com/scholarship/

AUGUST

MarvelOptics.com Scholarship Essay Contest
Eligibility: Full-time students attending an accredited four-year American university or college. Applicant must submit an essay or video answering the following prompt: How do you see the world?
Deadline: August 10 and January 5
Award: $1,500
Website: https://www.marveloptics.com/about-marvel-optics/scholarship-program/

Creative Outlook Cover Contest
Eligibility: Contest is open to current college level students, as well as high school students.
Contestant must submit an original piece of art.
Deadline: August 1
Award: $250
Website:
http://www.mymajors.com/blog/creativeoutlook/creative-outlook-cover-contest/

Guiding Light Scholarship
Eligibiity: Scholarship is open to legal U.S.
residents who are 18 years of age or older and is
or will be attending an accredited college or
university. Applicant must submit an essay on
who has influenced them.
Deadline: August 1
Award: $500
Website:
http://www.nfcperformance.com/guiding-light-scholarship

HBCU Connect Minority Scholarship Program
Eligibility: Minority students who are incoming or
current college students at Historically Black
Colleges and Universities (HBCUs).
Deadline: August 1
Award: $1,000
Website: http://hbcuconnect.com/scholarship/

Building Strong Foundations Scholarship
Eligibility: U.S. students who are 16 years of age
or older who are high school, undergraduate,
master degree, and adult learn students.
Applicant must submit application, personal
essay, and a short video.
Deadline: August 12
Award: $1,000
Website:
http://www.olshanfoundation.com/scholarships/

You, Me, and Poetry Scholarship Slam

Eligibility: Contest is open to individuals who are 25 years of age or younger and are current or former high school students who will attend or is attending college within the U.S. or its territories. Applicant must submit a poem on the theme: "What do poetry and being a poet mean to you?"
Deadline: August 17
Award: $1,000
Website: http://www.powerpoetry.org/poetry-slams/you-me-and-poetry-scholarship-slam-closed

Albertson & Davidson College Scholarship
Eligibility: Students currently attending or planning to attend an accredited United States college or university in the fall. Applicant must submit an essay on a given topic related to wills.
Deadline: August 24
Award: $2,500
Website:
http://www.aldavlaw.com/scholarship/

1000 Dreams Scholarship
Eligibility: Scholarship is open to high school and college women who can demonstrate financial need. Applicant will need to submit a completed application and at least one letter of recommendation.
Deadline: August and March
Award: Up to $1,000
Website:
https://www.growyourgiving.org/scholarships/1000-dreams-scholarship-fund

SEPTEMBER

Daily LineUp Scholarship Program
Eligibility: Scholarship is open to legal residents of the United States who are at least 16 years of age and are enrolled in an accredited post-secondary academic institution in the United States. Applicant must submit a short online form and answer three personal questions.
Deadline: September 1
Award: $1,000
Website: https://www.dailylineups.com/scholarship/

CIA Undergraduate Scholarship Program
Eligibility: Scholarship is open to high school seniors and college freshmen and sophomores who are at least 18 years of age and U.S. citizens. Applicant must have financial need. Applicants selected for the program will complete work sessions during each summer break in Washington, D.C. If selected, student will be given an annual salary, benefits package and up to $18,000 per calendar year for tuition, mandatory fees, books and supplies.
Deadline: September 23
Award: Annual salary; a benefits package that includes health insurance, life insurance, and retirement; and up to $18,000 per calendar year for tuition, mandatory fees, and books.
Website: https://www.cia.gov/careers/student-opportunities/undergraduate-scholarship-

program.html

QuestBridge
Eligibility: High school junior and seniors.
Deadline: September 27
Award: $1,000 to full tuition
Website: https://www.questbridge.org/

The LPGA Foundation
Eligibility: The LPGA Foundation administers
several scholarship programs for young women
who enjoy the game of golf and plan to attend
college in the fall. Qualifications for all
scholarships include strong academic programs,
community service, and recommendations.
Deadline: September 1
Award: $250 to $5,000
Website: www.lpgafoundation.org/scholarships

Hit the Books Scholarship
Eligibility: Students aged 18-25 who are enrolled
in an accredited college or university. Applicant
must submit a personal essay on the importance
of education in their lives and how the
scholarship money will assist their student goals.
Deadline: September 30
Award: Up to $500
Website:
http://www.coffeeforless.com/scholarship/

Siemens Foundation
Eligibility: Competition is open to individuals and
teams of up to three students in grades nine

through 12. Students are encouraged to do research in mathematics, engineering, biological, or physical science.
Deadline: September 20
Award: Up to $100,000
Website:
https://siemenscompetition.discoveryeducation.com/

Jackson White Criminal Law Bi-Annual Scholarship
Eligibility: Current undergraduate, graduate and law school students. Applicant must submit an essay on given topic related to the war on drugs.
Deadline: September 30
Award: $1,000
Website:
http://www.jacksonwhitelaw.com/criminal-defense-law/scholarship/

Odenza Marketing Group Scholarship
Eligibility: Students between the ages of 16 and 25 who are citizens of the United States and have a GPA of at least 2.5. Applicant must submit two essays on given topics.
Deadline: Sept 30
Award: $500
Website:
http://odenzascholarships.com/awards/8/eligibility_odenza_marketing_group_scholarship.php

OCTOBER

Horatio Alger Scholarship
Eligibility: High school senior with minimum 2.0 GPA, perseverance in overcoming adversity and critical financial need.
Deadline: October 25
Award: $6,000 to $25,000
Website: https://scholars.horatioalger.org/

Quest for Success Scholarship
Eligibility: Incoming or current college students who have a minimum cumulative GPA of 3.0 or above. Applicant must submit an essay on a given topic related to bicycle safety.
Deadline: October 31
Award: $500
Website:
http://www.bikeaccidentadvice.com/quest-success-scholarship/

Netfloor USA Scholarship
Eligibility: High school seniors, current undergraduate, and graduate students with at least a 3.0 GPA. Applicant must submit a personal essay and an essay on cable management.
Deadline: September 1
Award: $1,000
Website: https://www.netfloorusa.com/netfloor-usa-access-flooring-college-scholarship

Coca-Cola Scholars Foundation
Eligibility: Current high school or home-school seniors attending school in the U.S. Coca-Cola

Scholars are well-rounded, bright students who not only excel academically, but are also actively involved in their schools. These leaders are passionate and service-oriented, and demonstrate a sustained commitment to bettering their community.
Deadline: October
Award: $20,000
Website: http://www.coca-colascholarsfoundation.org/applicants/#programs

National Eagle Scouts Scholarships
Eligibility: High school seniors through college juniors who are Eagle Scouts.
Deadline: October 31
Award: $2,000 to $50,000
Website: www.universitylanguage.com/scholarships/competition

AXA Foundation Scholarships
Eligibility: High school students who demonstrate ambition and self-drive as evidenced by outstanding achievement in school, community or work-related activities.
Deadline: October 30
Award: $10,000 to $25,000
Website: https://us.axa.com/axa-foundation/about.html

Study Soup Future Innovator
Eligibility: The scholarship is available to High

School Senior students and students currently enrolled in college.
Deadline: October 1
Award: $2,000
Website: https://studysoup.com/scholarship

Al Young Sports Journalism Scholarship
Eligibility: Asian American students who are AAJA student members. Applicant must demonstrate journalistic excellence and a strong interest in pursuing sports journalism as a career.
Deadline: October 30
Award: Up to $2,500
Website: http://sportstaskforce.com/students-scholarship-opportunity/

Courage to Grow Scholarship
Eligibility: Juniors and seniors in high school or college students with a minimum GPA of 2.5. Applicant must explain in 250 words or less why they believe they should be awarded the scholarship.
Deadline: October 31
Award: $500
Website: http://couragetogrowscholarship.com/

NOVEMBER

Ronald Brown Scholars Program
Eligibility: Black/African American, must be rising high school junior or senior. Have a strong

academic record and demonstrated leadership and active involvement at school and/or in the community.
Deadline: November 1 and January 9
Award: $40,000 ($10,000/year)
Website: http://www.ronbrown.org

Geico Scholarship
Eligibility: Students enrolled full-time at an accredited four-year college or university in the United States who have attained sophomore or junior status. Applicant must have at least a 3.0 GPA, majoring in business, computer science, mathematics or a related program, and have demonstrated leadership on campus or in their community.
Deadline: November 17
Award: $2,500
Website:
https://www.geico.com/careers/students-and-grads/achievement-awards/program-overview/

Ford Foundation
Eligibility: Fellowship is open to all citizens, and permanent residents of the United States, as well as individuals granted deferred action status under the DACA program. Applicant must be enrolled or planning to enroll in an eligible research-based program leading to a Ph.D. or Sc.D. degree at a non-proprietary U.S. institution of higher education.
Deadline: November 17
Award: $24,000

Website:
http://sites.nationalacademies.org/PGA/FordFell
owships/PGA_171962

Golden Eagle Coins Scholarship Program
Eligibility: Must currently be enrolled as a high
school or college/university student within the
United States. Must have a cumulative GPA of at
least 3.0
Deadline: November 20
Award: $500
Website:
https://www.goldeneaglecoin.com/scholarship

Youth Noise
Eligibility: Students who are currently enrolled
in a high school, college, university, or trade
school are encouraged to submit their video
application.
Deadline: November 21
Award: $1,000
Website:
http://www.youthnoise.com/scholarship-
program

Jack Kent Cooke Foundation
Eligibility: High-achieving high school seniors
with financial need and seeking attendance to the
nation's best four-year colleges and universities.
To qualify, applicants must have a 3.5 GPA or
above and demonstrate significant unmet
financial need.
Deadline: November 3

Award: $30,000
Website: www.jkcf.org

Fix Your Skin Scholarship
Eligibility: Current high school and college students. Applicant must submit an essay on a given topic related to skincare.
Deadline: November 25
Award: $1,000
Website: http://fixyourskin.com/scholarship/

Prudential Spirit of Community Award
Eligibility: Students in middle school and high school who have made a difference through volunteering over the past year. To qualify, applicants must be in grades 5-12 as of November 4 and legal residents of any US state or Washington DC.
Deadline: November 4
Award: $1,000 to $5,000
Website: https://spirit.prudential.com/about/program-overview

Crowdifornia Essay Writing Competition
Eligibility: Legal residents of the 50 United States or the District of Columbia who are at least 18 years of age by the contest deadline and enrolled in a university or college, community college, or a trade or career-based school. Applicant must submit an essay that helps to raise awareness about population growth, immigration, and the trade-offs involved.

Deadline: November 30
Awards: Up to $1,500
Website: http://crowdifornia.org/

Voice of Democracy Scholarship Program
Eligibility: high school students in grades nine
through twelve and be enrolled in a public,
private, or parochial high school or home study
program in the United States or its territories.
Deadline: November 1
Award: $1,000 to $30,000
Website: https://www.vfw.org/VOD/

Harvey Fellows Program
Eligibity: This fellowship is for students enrolled
in or who have applied to a full-time graduate
program, demonstrate personal faith in Jesus
Christ and desire to serve and witness in His
name.
Deadline: November 1
Award: $12,000
Website:
http://msfdn.org/harveyfellows/overview/

DECEMBER

Footlocker Scholarship
Eligibility: High school senior with minimum 3.0
GPA entering college in the fall. Member of a
high school sports team or involved in afterschool
sports.
Deadline: December 16

Award: Up to $20,000
Website: www.footlockerscholarathletes.com

Best Fat Burner Scholarship
Eligibility: United States residents who are
enrolled as an undergraduate or graduate
student with a minimum GPA of 3.0. Applicant
must submit an essay on a given topic related to
weight loss.
Deadline: December 31 ·
Award: $500
Website:
http://bestfatburnersite.org/scholarship-
program/

Johnnie L. Cochran, Jr. Memorial Scholarship
Fund
Eligiblity: High school seniors and students
attending post-high school education. Winners
receive a one-time dispersal per winning entry.
Deadline: December 1
Award: $1,000
Website:
http://www.cochranfirmdc.com/scholarship

Burger King McLamore Foundation Scholarship
Program
Eligibility: All high school seniors and all
BURGER KING® restaurant, corporate and field
employees, their spouses and children in the
U.S., Canada and Puerto Rico are eligible to
apply.
Deadline: December 15

Award: $50,000/4 years
Website:
http://bkmclamorefoundation.org/who-we-are/application-information/

Ashley Soule Conroy Foundation Scholarship
Eligibility: Scholarship is open to students currently enrolled as an undergraduate student at a four-year college or university in the United States and are planning to participate in full-time study abroad for at least one full semester outside of the United States.
Deadline: July 1 and December 1
Award: $3,000
Website: http://www.ashleysfoundation.org/

Gen and Kelly Tanabe Scholarship
Eligibility: 9th-12th grade high school, college, or graduate student including adult students.
Deadline: December 31st
Award: $1,000
Website: http://gkscholarship.com/

Comcast Leaders and Achievers Scholarship Program
Eligibility: Scholarship is open to full-time high school seniors currently enrolled at a high school in a community serviced or approved by Comcast. Applicant must have a GPA of at least 2.8 and student must demonstrate leadership in school activities or work experiences.
Deadline: December 1
Award: $1,000

Website: http://corporate.comcast.com/news-information/news-feed/recognizing-the-best-and-brightest-nationwide

Gotch SEO Internet Marketing Scholarship
Eligibility: Marketing, Business, or Entrepreneurship. Applicant must be currently operating a side business while in college or have involvement in a family business.
Deadline: December 31
Award: $500
Website:
https://www.gotchseo.com/scholarship/

Get Up! Get Active!
Eligibility: Current college, graduate school, and adult learners. Applicant must submit three to five sentences answering one question related to money.
Deadline: December 31
Award: $1,000
Website:
http://www.getupgetactive.org/scholarship

100+ COLLEGES THAT OFFER FULL TUITION SCHOLARSHIPS

Tip: Use this list as a starting point for layer one in the Layering Technique ™.

ALABAMA
University of Alabama
Name of Scholarship: Academic Elite
Scholarships More
Info: http://scholarships.ua.edu/types/elite.html
Value: Full tuition + $8,500 per year + iPad
Determining Factors: Academics,
extracurriculars, service, and leadership
experience Minimum Requirements: 32 ACT or
1400 SAT, 3.8 GPA

Birmingham-Southern College
Name of Scholarship: Distinguished Scholars
Award More Info:
http://www.bsc.edu/fp/scholarships.cfm Value:
Up to full tuition Determining Factors: Academic
and extracurricular achievement

Troy University
Name of Scholarships: The Millennium Scholar's
Award and The Chancellor's Award More Info:

http://www.troy.edu/scholarships/index.html
Value: full tuition. Selection criteria: ACT or SAT scores and high school or junior college GPA.

CALIFORNIA

Scripps College

Name of Scholarship: New Generation Scholarship More Info: http://www.scholarships4school.com/scholarships/new-generation-scholarship.html Value: Full tuition + three flights home per year + one summer research stipend Determining Factors: Academic performance, personal achievement, recommendations, and involvement in community and school activities Minimum Requirements: Minimum weighted GPA of 4.0, minimum median SAT score of 1400

University of Southern California

Name of Scholarship: Mork Family Scholarship More Info: http://www.usc.edu/admission/undergraduate/docs/uscScholarships1415.pdf Value: Full tuition + $5,000 stipend Awards: 10 Name of Scholarship: Stamps Leadership Scholarship More Info:

http://www.usc.edu/admission/undergraduate/ docs/uscScholarships1415.pdf Value: Full tuition + $5,000 enrichment fund Awards: 5 Determining Factors: Academic achievement, talent, perseverance, innovation, involvement, and leadership Minimum Requirements: Average SAT and ACT scores in the top 1 to 2 percent of students nationwide Name of Scholarship: Trustee Scholarship More Info: http://www.usc.edu/admission/undergraduate/ docs/uscScholarships1415.pdf Value: Full tuition Awards: 100

Loyola Marymount University
Name of Scholarship: Trustee Scholarship More Info: http://financialaid.lmu.edu/prospective/scholar ships/lmuacademicscholarshipsforfreshmen/ Value: Full tuition + room and board Awards: 10 Determining Factors: Academic achievement Minimum Requirements: 3.6 GPA, SAT math and verbal 650 or ACT 29

Soka University of America
Name of Scholarship: Global Merit Scholarships More Info:

http://www.soka.edu/admission_aid/Financial_
Aid/merit_based_financial_aid.aspx Value: Full
tuition + transportation + books and supplies +
personal expenses + President's Scholars
Medallion at commencement + campus parking +
annual book allowance Minimum Requirements:
Subject to a continued GPA of 3.0 or higher

California Institute of Technology (Caltech)
Name of Scholarship: Stamps Leadership
Scholarship More Info:
https://www.finaid.caltech.edu/TypesofAid/gran
ts/Stamps Value: Full tuition Minimum
Requirements: Nomination, Must apply via non-
binding Early Action

University of California – Los Angeles
Name of Scholarship: Stamps Leadership
Scholarship More
Info: http://www.stampsfoundation.org/portfolio
s/university-of-california-los-angeles/ Value: Up
to full tuition + enrichment funds of up to
$12,000 Awards: 5 national awards, 5 for
California residents Determining Factors:
Leadership, scholarship, community service,
innovation Minimum Requirements: Nomination

University of California Irvine

Name of Scholarship: Regents Scholarship and Chancellor's Achievement Scholarship More Info: http://www.ofas.uci.edu/content/Scholarships.aspx Value: Full tuition Selection criteria: Comprehensive review of applicant pool to determine student's strength and breadth of academic preparation. Test scores and grades are also considered.

University of California Riverside

Name of Scholarship: Regents Scholarship More Info: http://financialaid.ucr.edu/scholarships/index.html Value: Full tuition + fees + Regents Scholars also receive priority course registration and are offered acceptance into the University Honors Program.

DELAWARE

University of Delaware

Name of Scholarship: Eugene DuPont Memorial Scholars More Info: http://www.udel.edu/admissions/pdf/DSDescriptions2012.pdf Value: Full tuition + room & board + $375 per semester for textbooks + $2,500 enrichment activities

DISTRICT OF COLUMBIA
American University
Name of Scholarship: Frederick Douglass
Scholars Program More Info:
http://www.american.edu/financialaid/fdsprogr
am.cfm Value: Full tuition + fees + room & board
+ books Determining Factors: "Preference will be
given to first-generation students as well as those
committed to working in communities of color in
the United States. " Most recipients have at least
a 3.2 GPA (unweighted) or 3.4 GPA (weighted)
and 1150 SAT (critical reading/math) or 25 ACT

Catholic University of America
Name of Scholarship: Archdiocesan Scholarship
More Info:
http://admissions.cua.edu/undergrad/finaid/sc
holarships_academic.html Value: Full tuition
Awards: 5 Determining Factors: Academic merit
Minimum Requirements: 3.8 GPA ,1450 SAT or
32 ACT, top 10% class rank

The George Washington University
Name of Scholarship: Presidential Academic
Scholarship More Info:

http://undergraduate.admissions.gwu.edu/schol arships Value: Full tuition

Howard University
Name of Scholarship: Presidential Scholarship
More Info:
http://www.howard.edu/financialaid/grants_sch olarships.htm Value: Full tuition + fees + room & board + $950 book voucher + laptop Determining Factors: Academic achievement Minimum Requirements: SAT 1500-1600 or ACT 34-36, GPA 3.75 Name of Scholarship: Founders Scholarship More Info:
http://www.howard.edu/financialaid/grants_sch olarships.htm Value: Full tuition+ fees + room & board + $500 book voucher Determining Factors: Academic achievement Minimum Requirements: SAT 1400-1490 or ACT 32-33, GPA 3.5 Name of Scholarship: Capstone Scholarship More Info:
http://www.howard.edu/financialaid/grants_sch olarships.htm Value: Full tuition + fees + room Determining Factors: Academic achievement Minimum Requirements: SAT 1300-1390 or ACT 29-31, GPA 3.25 Name of Scholarship: Legacy Scholarship More Info:
http://www.howard.edu/financialaid/grants_sch

olarships.htm Value: Tuition + fees Determining
Factors: Academic achievement Minimum
Requirements: SAT 1170-1290 or 26-28 ACT,
GPA 3.0 or ranked 1 or 2 in class

FLORIDA

University of Miami

Name of Scholarship: Hammond Scholarship
More Info:
http://www6.miami.edu/provost/oae/hammond
/index.html Value: Full tuition Determining
Factors: Academic excellence, a commitment to
personal goals, aspirations of continuing
education at the graduate level Name of
Scholarship: Singer Scholarship More Info:
http://www.miami.edu/admission/index.php/u
ndergraduate_admission/costsandfinancialresour
ces/scholarships/singer/ Value: Full tuition
Determining Factors: Exceptional qualities and
academic achievement Name of Scholarship:
Stamps Foundation Scholarship More Info:
http://www.miami.edu/admission/index.php/u
ndergraduate_admission/costsandfinancialresour
ces/scholarships/stamps_scholarships/ Value:
Full tuition + fees + room & board + textbooks +
enrichment stipend of $12,000 + leadership

programs Determining Factors: Exceptional qualities and academic achievement Minimum Requirements: Must apply early decision or early action

Rollins College

Name of Scholarship: Alfond Scholarship More Info: http://www.rollins.edu/finaid/as/alfond.html Value: Full tuition Awards: 10 Determining Factors: Overall academic record Minimum Requirements: Most winners have a minimum of 1420 SAT or 32 ACT and GPA above 3.6.

Stevenson University

Name of Scholarship: Presidential Fellowship More Info: http://www.stevenson.edu/admissions-aid/financial-aid-scholarships/types-of-aid/presidential-fellowship.html Value: Full Tuition Scholarship + $3,000 stipend Determining Factors: Commitment to academic excellence, proven leadership in school-based activities, community service, and/or athletics Minimum Requirements: Must apply by November 1st

Barry University

Name of Scholarship: Stamps Leadership Scholarship More Info: https://www.barry.edu/stamps/ Value: Tuition + room & board + $6,000 for study abroad or extraordinary learning experiences + faculty advisor + leadership opportunities Determining Factors: academics, leadership, and community service Minimum Requirements: 3.5 GPA

GEORGIA

Agnes Scott College

Name of Scholarship: Marvin B. Perry Presidential Scholarship More Info: http://www.agnesscott.edu/admission/financial-aid/agnes-scott-scholarships.html#perry Value: Full tuition + room & board Determining Factors: Academics, leadership, character, and personal achievement

Emory University

Name of Scholarship: Emory Scholars More Info: http://apply.emory.edu/apply/scholars.php Value: Up to full tuition + enrichment stipends Determining Factors: Academic achievement and extracurricular engagement Minimum Requirements: Application deadline November 15th

Georgia Institute of Technology

Name of Scholarship: Presidential Scholars More Info: http://www.psp.gatech.edu/ Value: Full tuition + room & board Determining Factors: Scholarship, leadership, progress, and service Minimum Requirements: Must apply by October 15th Name of Scholarship: Stamps Leadership Scholarship More Info: http://www.psp.gatech.edu/stamps-leadership-scholars Value: Full tuition + $4,000 for public service internship or research + study abroad or international experience funds up to $8,000 Awards: 5-6 national awards, 5-6 awards for Georgia residents Determining Factors: Academics, personal achievements, and leadership

University of Georgia

Name of Scholarship: Foundation Fellowship and Bernard Ramsey Honors Scholarship More Info: https://honors.uga.edu/c_s/scholarships/f_f/foundation_fellows.html Value: Full tuition

Determining Factors: Academic achievement,
intellectual drive, curiosity, record of leadership
and service, intellectual and cultural diversity
Minimum Requirements: Submit application by
November 3rd, 3.8 GPA, 2100 SAT or 31 ACT
Name of Scholarship: Stamps Leadership
Scholarship More Info:
http://www.stampsfoundation.org/portfolios/uni
versity-of-georgia-athens-ga/ Value: Full tuition +
$3,000 travel-study grant Determining Factors:
Overall achievement and leadership Minimum
Requirements: Must apply by mid-November

Oglethorpe University
Name of Scholarship: Jennett Scholars Program
More Info:
http://www.oglethorpe.edu/administrative/finan
cial_aid/scholarships.asp#JEO Value: Full
tuition + stipend for summer study abroad +
eligible for research stipend Awards: 5
Determining Factors: Academic achievement and
extracurricular/community involvement
Minimum Requirements: Must attend
Scholarship Weekend

Mercer University

Name of Scholarship: Stamps Leadership Scholarship More Info: http://www.stampsfoundation.org/2012/11/01/mercer-university-macon-ga/ Value: Full tuition + fees + room & board + $1,600 for books + iPad + $4,000 for enrichment activities Awards: 10 Determining Factors: leadership, perseverance, scholarship, service to humankind and innovation Minimum Requirements: Must submit application by November 1st

Morehouse College

Name of Scholarship: Stamps Leadership Scholarship More Info: http://www.morehouse.edu/admissions/ Value: Full tuition + $10,000 enrichment activities Awards: 5 Determining Factors: Overall achievement and leadership Minimum Requirements: 3.7 GPA, must apply by November 1st

HAWAII

University of Hawaii

Name of Scholarship: Regents' Scholarship More Info: http://www.hawaii.edu/offices/studentaffairs/sc

holarships/raps-overview.php Value: full tuition plus $4,000 per year and one time $2,000 travel grant Awards: 20 Determining Factors: Academic and extracurricular achievement Minimum Requirements: Regents': 3.5 high school academic GPA, 29 ACT or 1950 SAT. Presidential: 3.7 college GPA.

IOWA

Drake University

Name of Scholarship: National Alumni Scholarship and George A. Carpenter Scholarship More Info: http://www.drake.edu/admission/undergraduate/costsfinancialaid/typesofaid/scholarships/nationalalumni/ Value: Full tuition + fees + room & board Awards: 16 Determining Factors: Scholastic achievement, extracurricular and community activities, leadership, communication skills, and potential for contributing to the academic and extracurricular life Minimum Requirements: ACT 31, SAT 1380/1400 in math and critical reading, Top 5% or 3.8 GPA, submit application by December 1st

ILLINOIS
Knox College
Name of Scholarship: Presidential Scholarship
More Info:
http://www.knox.edu/admission/scholarships/academic-scholarships.html Value: Full tuition
Awards: 5

Illinois Institute of Technology
Name of Scholarship: Duchossois Leadership
Scholars More Info:
http://admissions.iit.edu/undergraduate/finances/duchossois-leadership-scholars-program
Value: Full tuition Minimum Requirements: none
Name of Scholarship: Camras Scholars Program
More
Info: http://admissions.iit.edu/undergraduate/finances/camras-scholars-program Value: Full
tuition + room & board + paid summer
experiences Determining Factors: Academics,
leadership, extracurricular activities,
communication skills, positive personality,
capacity for original through, sense of caring
Minimum Requirements: 3.5 GPA, ACT/SAT
scores in the top 10% nationally

University of Chicago

Name of Scholarship: Stamps Leadership Scholarship More Info: http://www.stampsfoundation.org/portfolios/university-of-chicago-chicago-il/ Value: Full tuition, room & board, $10,000 enrichment funds Determining Factors: Overall achievement and leadership

University of Illinois – Urbana Champaign

Name of Scholarship: Stamps Leadership Scholarship More Info: http://vcia.illinois.edu/giving/stamps.html Value: Full tuition + $12,000 for enrichment activities Awards: up to 5 Determining Factors: Leadership, overcoming obstacles, scholarship, service and innovation

INDIANA

Indiana University

Name of Scholarship: The Wells Scholarship Program More Info: http://www.indiana.edu/~wsp/ Value: Full tuition + fees + living stipend Awards: 18-22 Determining Factors: Academic achievement, leadership, extracurricular activities, community involvement, and character Minimum Requirements: Most nominees score 1400 or above on SAT or 32 on ACT have 3.9 GPA or higher, and graduate within the top 5% of their class. Scholars must be nominated by their school or the IUB admissions office.

Purdue University

Name of Scholarship: Stamps Leadership Scholarship More Info: http://www.stampsfoundation.org/portfolios/purdue-university-west-lafayette-in/ Value: Full tuition + $10,000 enrichment funds Determining Factors: Academics, leadership, extracurricular activities, and personal background and experiences Minimum Requirements: Submit application by November 1st

University of Notre Dame

Name of Scholarship: Stamps Leadership Scholarship More Info: http://www.stampsfoundation.org/portfolios/university-of-notre-dame/ Value: Full tuition + $12,000 enrichment funds + faculty and professional mentors Determining Factors: Leadership, perseverance, scholarship, service,

and innovation Minimum Requirements:
Nominated by admissions office

KANSAS
The University of Kansas
Name of Scholarships: Kansas National Merit
Scholarship, Kansas National Achievement
Scholarship, and Kansas National Hispanic
Scholarship More Info:
http://admissions.ku.edu/cs Value: Full tuition

KENTUCKY
Alice Lloyd College
The cost of education (tuition) is guaranteed for
all students from within the College's service area
due to the generosity of donors from across the
nation; however, students are expected to pay for
their living expenses (Room and Board) and the
student matriculation fee. More Info:
www.alc.edu

Berea College
Every admitted student gets a four-year tuition
scholarship. Housing is not included and
students work on campus in lieu of paying
tuition. More Info: https://www.berea.edu/

Transylvania University

Name of Scholarship: William T. Young
Scholarship More Info:
http://www.transy.edu/admission/scholarships
Value: Full tuition + fees Selection criteria:
Strong high school curriculum with a 4.0
average; ACT score minimum of 31 or SAT score
minimum of 1400 (out of 1600); excellent writing
ability; strong leadership experience and
community/high school involvement.

University of Kentucky

Name of Scholarship: Otis A. Singletary
Scholarship More Info:
http://www.uky.edu/Scholars/ Value: Full
tuition, room & board, stipend, iPad, $2,000
summer abroad stipend Minimum Requirements:
31 ACT or 1360 SAT and minimum unweighted
GPA of 3.5 Name of Scholarship: Presidential
Scholarship More
Info: http://www.uky.edu/financialaid/scholarsh
ip-incoming-freshmen Value: Full tuition
Minimum Requirements: "minimum test score of
31 ACT or 1360 SAT (Math + Reading) and
minimum unweighted GPA of 3.5 on a 4.0 scale"

University of Louisville
Name of Scholarship: Brown Fellows Program
More Info:
http://louisville.edu/admissions/aid/scholarshi
ps/jgb Value: Full tuition + room & board +
allowance for books + up to $5,000 in enrichment
funds Awards: 10 Determining Factors:
Academics, well-roundedness, leadership
potential Minimum Requirements: 31 ACT or
1360 SAT, 3.5 GPA, non-resident of Kentucky
(there are other scholarships for Kentucky
residents)

Morehead State University
Name of Scholarship: Presidential Scholarship
More Info:
http://www.moreheadstate.edu/scholarships/
Value: Full tuition + room and board. Selection
criteria: National Merit Scholar, National Merit
Finalist or Semi-Finalist; Kentucky Governor's
Scholars or Governor's School for the Art with at
least a 23 ACT composite; applicants with a high
school GPA of 3.75 or higher and a minimum 28
ACT composite; or a valedictorian/salutatorian
from an accredited Kentucky higher with a
minimum 28 ACT composite.

138

Name of Scholarship: Commonwealth Scholarship Value: Full tuition. Selection criteria: Candidates must be admitted to MSU as an entering freshman with a minimum admission index of 600; and be a legal resident of Kentucky; and have a minimum 20 ACT composite; and agree to maintain continuous residency is campus housing.

LOUISIANA
Tulane University
Name of Scholarship: Dean's Honor Scholarship More Info: http://admission.tulane.edu/aid/merit.php Value: Full tuition Awards: 75 Determining Factors: General achievement and a creative project Minimum Requirements: Must submit application by November 15th via Early Action Name of Scholarship: Paul Tulane Scholarship More Info: http://admission.tulane.edu/aid/merit.php Value: Full tuition Awards: 50 Determining Factors: General Achievement Minimum Requirements: Must submit application by November 15th via Early Action Name of Scholarship: Stamps-Tulane Scholarship More

Info: http://admission.tulane.edu/aid/merit.php
Value: Full tuition + enrichment funding Awards:
5 Determining Factors: Academics, leadership,
perseverance, service and innovation Minimum
Requirements: Must apply for Dean's Honor
Scholarship and nominated from that pool

Louisiana State University

Name of Scholarship: Stamps Leadership
Scholarship More Info:
https://www.honors.lsu.edu/prospective-
students/admissions/scholarships/stamps-
leadership-scholarships Value: Full tuition + up
to $14,000 enrichment expenses Minimum
Requirements: Selected from students admitted
to the honors program, 33 ACT, 1440 SAT, 3.0
GPA

MAINE

Husson College

Distinguished Scholar Scholarship provides 10-
15 awards per year for full tuition. Selected by
Admission Office and awarded only to first year
students who are Validictorians or Salutatorians
in their class. No special application needed.
More Info: http://www.husson.edu/

MARYLAND

University of Maryland – College Park

Name of Scholarship: Banneker/Key Scholarship
More Info: http://www.bannekerkey.umd.edu/
Value: Up to full tuition + room & board + book
allowance Awards: 150 Determining Factors:
Academics, leadership Minimum Requirements:
Must be admitted to the Honors College Name of
Scholarship: Stamps Leadership Scholarship
More Info:
http://www.bannekerkey.umd.edu/stamps.php
Value: Tuition + room & board + book allowance
+ up to $5,000 enrichment funds Awards: 2-3
Determining Factors: Academic leadership
Minimum Requirements: Must be admitted to the
Honors College, admitted through the same pool
as Banneker/Key Scholarship

**Johns Hopkins University, Whiting School of
Engineering**

Two four-year full tuition scholarships are
awarded each year to entering students by the
Dean of Engineering and the Admissions
Committee. The awards are for undergraduate
study in any engineering major. More Info:

http://grad.jhu.edu/cost-of-attendance/

Loyola College in Maryland
Name of Scholarship: Presidential Scholarship.
10 to 15 full tuition scholarships awarded
annually. More Info:
http://www.loyola.edu/admission/undergraduat
e
Name of Scholarship: Marion Burk Knott
Scholarship. 1 full-tuition scholarhip award.
More Info:
http://www.loyola.edu/admission/undergraduat
e

Stevenson University
Name of Scholarship: Presidential Fellowship
More
Info: http://www.stevenson.edu/admissions-
aid/scholarships-financial-aid/types-of-
aid/presidential-fellowship/ Value: Full tuition +
$3,000 for faculty-led trip Determining Factors:
Commitment to academic excellence, proven
leadership in school-based activities, community
service, and/or athletics Minimum Requirements:
Must complete application by November 1st

MASSACHUSETTS

Boston College

Name of Scholarship: Presidential Scholars Program More Info: http://www.bc.edu/centers/psp// Value: Full tuition Awards: 15 Determining Factors: Academic record, community service, and leadership Minimum Requirements: Apply Early Action by November 1st

Boston University

Name of Scholarship: Trustee Scholarship More Info: http://www.bu.edu/admissions/apply/costs-aid-scholarships/scholarships/trustee/ Value: Full Tuition + fees Awards: 20 Determining Factors: Academics, service, and extracurricular activities Minimum Requirements: Apply before December 1st, nomination from high school

Northeastern University

Name of Scholarship: University Scholars More Info: http://www.northeastern.edu/universityscholars/prospective-scholars/ Value: Full tuition Awards: 120 Determining Factors: Academic achievement, creativity, energy, ideas, ambition to innovate, curiosity, entrepreneurial spirit, vision, confidence, maturity, resourcefulness, passion to make a positive difference, and strong character.

University of Detroit Mercy
Name of Scholarship: Phi Theta Kappa Scholarship and Jesuit Founders Scholarship More Info: http://www.udmercy.edu/apply/financial-aid/scholarships/index.htm Value: Full tuition Selection criteria: Minimum 3.5+ GPA, 24+ transferable credits, scholarship essay, 2 letters of recommendation.

MICHIGAN
Aquinas College
Several full tuition scholarships are awarded each year by the Admissions Office. The Byrne Scholarship also includes room and board. More Info: https://www.aquinas.edu

Southwestern Michigan College
Name of Scholarship: Award of Distinction More Info: https://www.swmich.edu/financialaid

Value: Full tuition + fees. Selection criteria: High school cumulative GPA of 3.75 or higher

Michigan State University
Name of Scholarship: Alumni Distinguished Scholarship More Info: http://admissions.msu.edu/finances/scholarships_merit.asp Value: Full tuition + fees + room & board + $1,000 stipend annually Awards: 15 Determining Factors: Academic performance and participation in the MSU Alumni Distinguished Scholarship competition Minimum Requirements: Must apply by November 1st and complete an examination Name of Scholarship: Distinguished Freshman Scholarship More Info: http://admissions.msu.edu/finances/scholarships_merit.asp Value: Full tuition + fees Awards: 20 Determining Factors: Academic Performance and participation in the MSU Alumni Distinguished Scholarship competition Minimum Requirements: Must apply by November 1st and complete an examination

MISSISSIPPI
University of Mississippi
Name of Scholarship: Stamps Leadership

Scholarship More Info:
http://www.stampsfoundation.org/portfolios/uni
versity-of-mississippi-university-ms/ Value: Full
tuition + $12,000 enrichment stipend
Determining Factors: Academic achievement,
leadership, and service

MISSOURI
Saint Louis University
Name of Scholarship: Presidential Scholarship
More Info: http://www.slu.edu/undergraduate-
admission/scholarships-and-financial-
aid/presidential-scholarship Value: Full tuition +
up to $1,200 in enrichment funding Minimum
Requirements: GPA 3.85, weighted or
unweighted, 30 ACT or 1330 SAT

Washington University in St. Louis
Name of Scholarship: John B. Ervin's Scholar
Program More Info:
http://admissions.wustl.edu/scholarships-
financial-aid/Freshman-Academic-Scholarship-
Fellowship-Programs/Pages/John-B-Ervin-
Scholars-Program.aspx Value: Full tuition +
$2,500 stipend annually Determining Factors:
"Applicants should excel academically, challenge

themselves, demonstrate initiative and leadership in their communities, bring diverse groups together, commit to community service, serve historically underprivileged populations, and/or persevere through challenging circumstances." Name of Scholarship: Annika Rodriguez Scholars Program More Info: http://admissions.wustl.edu/scholarships-financial-aid/Freshman-Academic-Scholarship-Fellowship-Programs/Pages/Annika-Rodriguez-Scholars-Program.aspx Value: Full tuition + $2,500 stipend per year Determining Factors: "Awards are based on academic achievement (strong grades and SAT or ACT scores), a commitment to serving historically underprivileged populations, the ability to bring diverse people together, application answers and essay, and recommendations received as part of the admission application." Name of Scholarship: Danforth Scholars Program More Info: http://admissions.wustl.edu/scholarships-financial-aid/Freshman-Academic-Scholarship-Fellowship-Programs/Pages/The-Danforth-Scholars-Program.aspx Value: Full tuition Determining Factors: "In addition to outstanding academic performance, the committee in interested in activities that illustrate the candidate's exceptional commitment to community service, high moral character, and similar qualities that exemplify the Danforths' legacy at Washington University. The selection committee finds it helpful to learn of specific examples of leadership, academic, and personal achievements that set this student apart from his or her peers." Minimum Requirements: Must be nominated by person with extensive knowledge of student Name of Scholarship: Stamps Leadership Scholarship More Info: http://admissions.wustl.edu/scholarships-financial-aid/Freshman-Academic-Scholarship-Fellowship-Programs/Pages/Stamps-Leadership-Scholarships.aspx Value: Full tuition + fees + room & board + supplies + $10,000 enrichment fund Determining Factors: Academic achievement, leadership, perseverance, scholarship, service and innovation

NEW JERSEY
Stevens Institute of Technology
Name of Scholarship: The Ann P. Neupauer Scholarship More
Info: http://www.stevens.edu/sit/financial-

aid/merit-scholarships Value: Full tuition
Awards: 30

Ramapo College

Name of Scholarship: Presidential Scholarship
and Ramapo Scholarship More Info:
http://www.ramapo.edu/admissions/financial-
aid-tuition/scholarships/ Selection criteria:
Incoming freshmen only. Top 10% of high school
graduating class and have at least a 1250
combined on the Critical Reading and Math
portions of the SAT.

NEW MEXICO

New Mexico State University

Name of Scholarship: President's Associates
Honors Scholarship More Info:
http://admissions.nmsu.edu/scholarships/
Value: 12-15 full tuition and fees scholarships,
plus a $1,750/semester stipend. Selection
criteria: New Mexico high school graduates (high
school diploma or NM GED); 3.75 GPA with 28
ACT/1240 SAT or 3.5 GPA with 30 ACT/1320
SAT. Must submit online application by mid-
January.

See the website for a full list of all full tuition scholarships
http://admissions.nmsu.edu/scholarships/

NEW YORK
University of Buffalo
Name of Scholarship: Presidential Scholarship
More Info:
http://admissions.buffalo.edu/costs/meritscholarships.php Value: Full tuition + fees + housing + board and books Minimum Requirements: Unweighted high school average of 95 and SAT critical reading and math score of at least 1470 or ACT score of 33

Fordham University
Name of Scholarship: Presidential Scholarship
More Info:
http://www.fordham.edu/admissions/undergraduate_admiss/financing/financial_aid_facts_31974.asp Value: Full Tuition + room Awards: 20 Determining Factors: Academic achievement in high school, test scores, and personal characteristics

Macaulay Honors College at CUNY

Students must meet CUNY NYS residency requirements for in state tuition to receive the full tuition scholarship. More Info: http://macaulay.cuny.edu

Syracuse University

Name of Scholarship: Coronat Scholars More Info: http://www.syr.edu/financialaid/scholarships/su_scholarships_list/coronat_scholars.html Value: Full tuition + one paid study abroad trip + funding for summer experience + admission to honors program Determining Factors: Academic achievement, leadership, and service activities

University of Rochester

Name of Scholarship: Renaissance & Global Scholarships More Info: http://enrollment.rochester.edu/admissions/res/pdf/rens.pdf Value: Full tuition + individual mentoring Awards: 20 Determining Factors: Academic Curiosity and Excellence and Social Awareness and Involvement

Niagara University

Name of Scholarship: Niagara University Honors

Scholarship More Info:
http://www.niagara.edu/scholarships-and-grants/

St. Lawrence University
Name of Scholarship: Trustee Scholarship More Info: http://www.stlawu.edu/admissions/merit-scholarships Value: Full tuition Determining Factors: Academic excellence, character and leadership

SUNY Alfred College
Name of Scholarship: Distinguished Scholars Program: Excellence in Education Scholarship More Info: https://www.alfredstate.edu/financial-aid/scholarships/distinguished-scholar-program Value: Full tuition + room & board Determining Factors: Minimum Requirements: GPA of 94 or better through junior year; at least a 1250 (critical reading and math) combined SAT or 28 composite ACT score is required

NORTH CAROLINA
Davidson College
Name of Scholarship: John Montgomery Belk

Scholarship More Info:
http://www.davidson.edu/admission-and-
financial-aid/financial-
aid/scholarships/nomination-scholarships
Value: Full tuition + $6,000 for summer
experiences Awards: 8 Determining Factors:
Academic achievement, character, leadership,
and service Minimum Requirements: School
nomination

Duke University

Name of Scholarship: Robertson Scholars More
Info: http://robertsonscholars.org/ Value: Full
tuition + fees + room & board + funding for up to
three summer experiences Determining Factors:
Purposeful leadership, intellectual curiosity,
strength of character, and collaborative spirit

University of North Carolina – Chapel Hill

Name of Scholarship: Morehead-Cain Scholars
More Info: http://www.moreheadcain.org/ Value:
Full tuition + room & board + books + laptop +
funding for research and summer opportunities
Minimum Requirements: All students from
Canada, Great Britain, and North Carolina can
apply. All other students must come from a

designated nomination school or have your school register to become a nomination school. You can find a list of current nominating schools here: http://www.moreheadcain.org/nominating-schools/ Name of Scholarship: Robertson Scholars More Info: http://robertsonscholars.org/ Value: Full tuition + fees + room and board + funding for up to three summer experiences Determining Factors: Purposeful leadership, intellectual curiosity, strength of character, and collaborative spirit

North Carolina State University
Name of Scholarship: Park Scholarship More Info: http://park.ncsu.edu/ Value: Full tuition + fees + room & board + books & supplies + travel + laptop + personal expenses + admission to University Scholars Program Determining Factors: "Academic merit, exemplary character, exceptional potential for leadership, and the sense of promise that they may one day make contributions of enduring importance to the betterment of the human condition" Minimum Requirements: Endorsement by school or filled out self-endorsement form

Wake Forest University

Name of Scholarship: Nancy Susan Reynolds Scholarship More Info: http://groups.wfu.edu/debate/Recruiting/FINANCIALAIDSCHOLARSHIPS.html Value: All expenses associated with attending college + stipend Minimum Requirements: Must apply by December 1st Determining Factors: Scholarship, achievement, and personal interviews Name of Scholarship: Stamps Leadership Scholarship More Info: http://www.stampsfoundation.org/portfolios/wake-forest-winston-salem-nc/ Value: Full tuition + enrichment stipend Awards: 5 Determining Factors: Educational achievements, academic motivation, maturity and character

University of North Carolina – Charlotte

Name of Scholarship: Levine Scholars Program More Info: http://levinescholars.uncc.edu/ Value: Full tuition + room & board + fees + laptop + summer experience funding + study abroad + $8,000 grant to implement a service project + membership to Honors College Determining Factors: Scholarship, ethical leadership, and civic engagement

North Carolina A&T State University

Name of Scholarship: National Alumni Association Scholarship More Info: http://www.ncat.edu/admissions/financial-aid/aid/scholarships/fresh-students.html Value: Full tuition + fees + room & board and books Determining Factors: Academic talent and ability Minimum Requirements: Minimum qualifications include having a 3.0 or higher high school GPA and a 1000 or higher SAT (verbal and math only) or 22 ACT score. Name of Scholarship: Lewis and Elizabeth Dowdy Scholarship More Info: http://www.ncat.edu/admissions/financial-aid/aid/scholarships/fresh-students.html Value: full tuition, fees, room & board Minimum Requirements: 3.75 or higher GPA and a 1200 SAT (verbal and math) or 26 ACT score

Salem College

Name of Scholarship: Robert E. Elberson Scholarship More Info: http://www.salem.edu/admissions/scholarships# Value: Full tuition + room & board + semester of study abroad in England Name of Scholarship: Chatham/Davis/Weyand/Womble/Whitaker

Scholarships More
Info: http://www.salem.edu/admissions/scholar
ships# Value: Full tuition Awards: 10-15
Determining Factors: Academic performance,
evidence of leadership, responsibility, concern for
others, initiative, motivation, creativity,
resourcefulness, and vigor

OHIO

Bluffton University

Two full-tuition scholarships are awarded each
year by admissions and financial aid. More Info:
http://www.bluffton.edu

Miami University

Name of Scholarship: University Merit
Scholarship More Info:
http://miamioh.edu/admission/merit-grid/
Value: Up to full tuition Determining Factors:
Academic achievement and holistic review of
application Minimum Requirements: 32 ACT or
1400 SAT, 3.5 GPA   Name of Scholarship:
Stamps Leadership Scholarship More Info:
http://www.miami.edu/admission/index.php/u
ndergraduate_admission/costsandfinancialresour
ces/scholarships/stamps_scholarships/ Value:

Full tuition + fees + room & board + textbooks + $12,000 enrichment funds

Ohio State University

Name of Scholarship: Eminence Scholarship More Info: http://honors-scholars.osu.edu/honors/eminence Value: Full Ride + $3,000 enrichment Determining Factors: Academic achievement, contribution to school and local community, and leadership Minimum Requirements: Most recipients typically rank in the top three percent of their graduating classes and have an ACT composite score of 34 or higher or combined SAT Critical Reading and Math score of 1520 or higher."

Denison University

Name of Scholarship: Mary Carr Endowed Scholarship, Dr. Betty Lovelace Scholarship, and Dr. Desmond Hamlet Scholarship More Info: http://denison.edu/campus/admissions/financial-aid/types-of-aid Value: Full tuition Determining Factors: Academic achievement, outstanding leadership and personal merit

Hiram College

Name of Scholarship: Trustee Scholarship More Info: http://www.hiram.edu/admission/undergraduate/scholarships-and-grants Value: Full tuition Determining Factors: Academic achievement Minimum Requirements: GPA 3.8 and ACT 28 or SAT 1260

The Ohio State University at Marion

Name of Scholarship: Dean's Scholar and Marion Scholarhship More Info: http://osumarion.osu.edu/academics/majors/engineering/scholarships.html Value: Full tuition + fees + books for Engineering students

Oberlin College

Name of Scholarship: Stamps Leadership Scholarship More Info: http://new.oberlin.edu/office/financial-aid/prospective-students/outside-scholarships.dot Value: Full tuition + fees + $5,000 enrichment funding Determining Factors: Excellence in academic and/or musical talent

University of Toledo

Name of Scholarship: Presidential Scholarships
More Info:
http://www.utoledo.edu/admission/freshman/s
cholarships/2017/
Value: Full tuition + fees + room and board +
$3,000 stipend

OREGON
Lewis and Clark College
Name of Scholarship: Barbara Hirschi Neely
Scholarship More Info:
https://www.lclark.edu/offices/financial_aid/me
rit_scholarships/ Value: Full tuition + fees +
$2,000 stipend Determining Factors: Academic
achievement and distinctive personal
accomplishment. "Special preference is given to
students committed to studying the sciences, or
students with an unusually keen interest in
intercultural and international issues"

Pacific Northwest College of Art
Name of Scholarship: The Dorothy Lemeison
Scholarship More Info:
http://pnca.edu/admissions/fa/c/scholarships
Value: Full tuition Selection: ne scholarship for
full cost-of-attendance is awarded each year by

the Admissions Office. The scholarship is renewable for up to four years. Selection criteria: Awarded to a student who shows exceptional promise as indicated by academic history, admissions essays and portfolio.

PENNSYLVANIA
Albright College
High achieving students with demonstrated leadership and commitment to service add to the Albright community in significant ways. To reward those students for their good work, Albright offers a variety of Scholarships.
More Info:
http://www.albright.edu/admission/scholarship s.html

Arcadia University
Name of Scholarship: President's Scholarship
More Info:
http://www.arcadia.edu/Scholarships-and-Grants/ Value: Full tuition Determining Factors: Academic excellence, outstanding leadership and community and volunteer service

Curtis Institute of Music

Since 1928 Curtis has maintained an all-scholarship policy. The Curtis Institute of Music provides merit-based, full-tuition scholarships to all undergraduate and graduate students, regardless of their financial situation.
More Info: www.curtis.edu

University of Pittsburgh
Name of Scholarship: University Academic Scholarship More Info: https://oafa.pitt.edu/learn-about-aid/academic-scholarships/ Value: Up to full tuition Determining Factors: Academic achievement is the primary factor. Activities outside of the classroom such as leadership positions, athletics, community service, etc. are reviewed as a secondary consideration. Minimum Requirements: Most recipients have a minimum SAT I score of 1450 (math and critical reading scores only) or 33 ACT composite score, an 'A' average, and a top 5% class rank"

Elizabethtown College
Name of Scholarship: Stamps Leadership Scholarship More Info: http://www.etown.edu/admissions/stamps.aspx

Value: Full tuition + $4,000 enrichment funds + personal mentor Determining Factors: Leadership, perseverance, scholarship, service, and innovation

RHODE ISLAND
Providence College
Name of Scholarship: Liberal Arts Honors Scholarship More Info: http://www.providence.edu/financial-aid/applying-aid/pages/institutional-merit-based.aspx Value: Up to full tuition (though most offers are between 40-60% of tuition) Determining Factors: Academic achievement is primary consideration but will also look at extracurricular activities and personal accomplishments.

SOUTH CAROLINA
Clemson University
Name of Scholarship: National Scholars More Info: http://www.clemson.edu/academics/programs/national-scholars/ Value: Full tuition Awards: 40 Determining Factors: Outstanding academic achievement (average scholar achieved 1500 on SAT math & verbal or 34 ACT and was ranked in

top 1% of class), leadership, service, and
extracurricular involvement

Furman University
Name of Scholarship: Herman W. Lay
Scholarship More Info:
http://www2.furman.edu/admission/EngageFur
man/FinancialInformation/Pages/Merit-based-
scholarships.aspx Value: Full tuition + fees +
room & board Awards: 4 Determining Factors:
Academic Achievement (most recipients have
above 32 on the ACT or above 1400 on the SAT),
extracurricular involvement, and personal
achievement Name of Scholarship: James B.
Duke Scholarship More Info:
http://www2.furman.edu/admission/EngageFur
man/FinancialInformation/Pages/Merit-based-
scholarships.aspx Value: Full tuition Awards: 10
Determining Factors: Awards (most recipients
have above 32 on the ACT or above 1400 on the
SAT), extracurricular involvement, and personal
achievement

Wofford College
Name of Scholarship: The Richardson Family
Scholarship More Info:

http://www.wofford.edu/richardsonScholars/scholarshipInfo/ Value: Full tuition + fees + room & board + laptop + summer internships plus one overseas experience + January experience Determining Factors: Leadership, academic achievement and character Minimum Requirements: Nomination by school. Top 10 percent of the class and combined score of 1250 (critical reading and math) on the PSAT or SAT or a 28 on the ACT

University of South Carolina

Name of Scholarships: McNair Scholars and Carolina Scholars More Info: http://www.sc.edu/financialaid/scholarships/general_university_scholarships/default.html Value: Full tuition Selection criteria: Superior scholastic ability and achievement, leadership potential, and character. Financial need is not a consideration. Typical candidates rank at the top of their class and present SAT scores above 1300.

TENNESSEE

Rhodes College

Name of Scholarship: Bellingrath Scholarship More Info:

http://www.rhodes.edu/finaid/608.asp Value: Full tuition Awards: 1 Determining Factors: Academic achievement and personal achievements

Vanderbilt University

Name of Scholarship: Ingram Scholarship More Info: http://www.vanderbilt.edu/scholarships/ingram.php Value: Full tuition + stipends for summer projects Determining Factors: Commitment to community service, strength of personal character, and leadership potential Name of Scholarship: Cornelius Vanderbilt Scholarship Program More Info: http://www.vanderbilt.edu/scholarships/signature.php Value: Full tuition + stipend for one study abroad or research experience Determining Factors: Academic achievement, intellectual promise, and leadership and contribution outside the classroom

TEXAS

University of Texas at Austin

Name of Scholarship: 40 Acres Scholarship More Info:

http://scholarships.texasexes.org/scholarships/forty-acres-scholars/ Value: Full tuition + fees + books + living stipend + support for enrichment activities

Southern Methodist University

Name of Scholarship: President's Scholar Program More Info: http://www.smu.edu/Academics/PS/Benefits Value: Full tuition + fees + travel expenses and tuition for study abroad Determining Factors: Academic achievement and a demonstrated commitment to engagement in school and/or community activities Minimum Requirements: Exceptional achievement on the ACT or SAT, a minimum of 20 high school academic units in a challenging curriculum, including AP/IB and honors courses, two years of a single foreign language, and advanced coursework in math and science, and a high school rank in the top 10 percent of the graduating class

Southwestern University

Name of Scholarship: Brown Scholars More Info: http://www.southwestern.edu/aid/types/scholarships/merit.php Value: Full tuition Minimum

Requirements: Top 5% of their high school class (or if high school does not rank, have the equivalent of a 3.8 GPA on a 4.0 scale). Students must score at least a 1400 on the SAT (critical reading and math) or 31 on the ACT

Texas Christian University
Name of Scholarship: Chancellor's Scholarship
More Info:
http://www.chancellor.tcu.edu/scholars.asp
Value: Full tuition Awards: 43 Determining Factors: Academic achievement is the primary factor (SAT score average of recipients is 2190. ACT is 33), and leadership accomplishments, service records, and extracurricular activities are also considered.

University of Houston
Name of Scholarship: Tier One Scholarship More Info: http://www.uh.edu/tieronescholars/ Value: Full tuition + fees + two years room & board + stipend for research and study abroad + membership to Honors College + priority registration for classes Minimum Requirements: Minimum SAT of 1300 on the critical reading and math sections (29 ACT composite), rank in the

top 10 percent of high school class

University of Texas at Dallas

Name of Scholarship: The McDermott Scholars Program More Info: http://www.utdallas.edu/mcdermott/ Value: Full tuition + fees + $1,200 stipend per month to cover room, board, and living expenses + $1,000 annual book stipend + international experience up to $12,000 + professional development experience up to $3,000 + paid travel home twice a year for domestic students and once a year for international students Awards: 24 Determining Factors: Exceptional academic performance (most recipients have 1400 or higher on the two part SAT (verbal and math) and a class rank in the top 5% of their high school class, community volunteerism and leadership in school, broad and eclectic interests in science, literature, and the arts, social skills to interact easily with adults as well as peers.

VIRGINIA

University of Richmond

Name of Scholarship: Richmond Scholars More Info:

http://scholars.richmond.edu/about/index.html
Value: Full tuition + $3,000 for enrichment
activities + priority course registration +
guaranteed housing Determining Factors:
Outstanding and engaged scholarship, desire to
be at the forefront in the creation and discovery
of new knowledge, leadership skills, desire to be a
leader in service to society, broad worldview,
excitement about learning from people who are
different from themselves in a diverse community
of scholars, recognition of the importance of
personal integrity and ethical decision making,
enthusiastic pursuit of self-improvement, desire
to make the most of opportunities presented,
exceptional talent in artistic expression.
University of Virginia
Name of Scholarship: Jefferson Scholarship More
Info: http://www.jeffersonscholars.org/ Value:
Full tuition + fees + room & board+ books +
personal expenses

Washington and Lee
Name of Scholarship: Johnson scholarship More
Info: http://www.wlu.edu/johnson-program/the-
johnson-scholarship Value: Full tuition + room &
board + $7,000 to support summer experiences

Determining Factors: Academic and personal accomplishments, essays, performance at in-person scholarship competition (travel expenses are paid by the university for all finalists)

WEST VIRGINIA
Marshall University
Name of Scholarship: Society of Yeager Scholars
More Info: http://www.marshall.edu/sfa/ Value: Full tuition + fees + room & board + books & supplies + $8,500 for study abroad. Minimum requirements: ACT composite score of 30 or a minimum SAT score of 1340 (math and critical reading).
Name of Scholarship: John Marshal Scholars.
More Info: http://www.marshall.edu/sfa/ Value: Full tuition + fees + $1,250 stipend Determining Factors: ACT composite score of 30 or SAT score of 1320 or higher and a 3.5 GPA. Awards are not competitive. John Marshall Scholarships are automatic if admittance and test scores/high school grades are received by the deadline.

WISCONSIN
Carthage College
Name of Scholarship: Presidential Scholarship

More Info:
http://www.carthage.edu/admissions/scholarships/presidential/ Value: Up to full tuition + room & board

COMMUNITY SERVICE SCHOLARSHIPS

AXA Achievement Community Scholars Program

With the mission of bringing access to higher education into every community nationwide, the AXA Foundation distributes up to 12 AXA Achievement Community Scholarships for $2,000 each to high school seniors who demonstrate strong ambition, determination, respect, academic achievement, and commitment to volunteer services. In addition, the program selects one outstanding student from each state, the District of Columbia, and Puerto Rico to receive a one-time community service scholarship for $10,000.
Website: https://us.axa.com/axa-foundation/about.html

Bonner Scholars Program

As a national philanthropic organization created by investor Bertram F. Bonner and his wife Corella in Princeton, New Jersey, the Bonner Scholars Program provides four-year $4,000 community service scholarships for up to 1,500 students enrolled at one of the 22 participating

universities across the United States annually. In return for the financial support, recipients are required to commit at least 10 hours each week to volunteer work and participate in the foundation's summer community service internship experience.
Website: http://www.bonner.org/

Buick Achievers Scholarship
The Buick Achievers Program is for high school seniors or undergraduates who are leaders in the classroom and in the community. You should be majoring in engineering, technology, design or business and have an interest in the automotive industry.50 renewable scholarship up to $25,000 per year.
Website: http://buickachievers.com/

Davison Institute
The Davidson Fellows Scholarship awards $50,000, $25,000 and $10,000 scholarships to extraordinary young people, 18 and under, who have completed a significant piece of work. Application categories are Science, Technology, Engineering, Mathematics, Literature, Music, Philosophy and Outside the Box. Davidson

Fellows are honored every year in Washington, D.C. with Congressional meetings and a special reception.
Website:
http://www.davidsongifted.org/Fellows-Scholarship

Echoing Green Climate Change Fellowship Program
In partnership with the ZOOM Foundation, the Echoing Green Climate Change Fellowship Program provides an $80,000 stipend with health insurance to individuals who agree to participate in one year of professional development in community or humanitarian public service within the developing countries of the world. Website:
http://www.echoinggreen.org/fellowship

Elks National Foundation Scholarship Program
The Elks National Foundation awards 500 four-year scholarships to the highest-rated applicants. US citizens who have shown leadership, scholarship, and financial need can apply. There are 2 awards of $50,000, 2 awards of $40,000, 2 awards of $30,000, 14 awards of $20,000, and 480 awards of $4,000.

Website:
http://www.elks.org/scholars/scholarships/mvs
.cfm

GE-Reagan Foundation Scholarship
The GE-Reagan Foundation Scholarship Program
honors the legacy and character of our nation's
40th President by rewarding college-bound
students who demonstrate exemplary leadership,
drive, integrity, and citizenship with financial
assistance to pursue higher education. Through
the generous support of GE, this national
program annually awards $10,000 renewable
scholarships to numerous students.
Website:
https://www.reaganfoundation.org/education/sc
holarship-programs/

Heart of America Christopher Reeves Award
For those with the tendency to swoop in to help
others like Superman, the Heart of America
Christopher Reeve Award presents $1,000
annually to extraordinary middle or high school
students who have demonstrated a tremendous
amount of compassion and service to his or her
local community. In order to be selected for the

scholarship, eligible nominees must provide information about recent community service efforts with supporting documentation and professional reference letters.

Website:

https://theheartofamerica.wufoo.com/forms/w1i a5cs00bmc43b/

Or www.heartofamerica.org

Montage Memory Makers Scholarships

Montage Hotels & Resorts is in search of young community leaders between the ages of 13-17 years old who are making the world a better place. A $10,000 scholarship towards an accredited college or university, two-night stay at one of our Montage Hotels & Resorts locations and winners will be included in the spring issue of Montage Magazine.

Website:

https://www.montagehotels.com/montage-memory-makers-scholarship/

Prudential Spirit of Community Award

Sponsored by Prudential and the National Association of Secondary School Principals (NASSP), the Prudential Spiritual of Community

Awards are granted for $1,000 to $5,000 each to high school seniors accepted for enrollment in an undergraduate degree program who have continually engaged in community volunteer service. Eligible candidates are required to complete an application, write a personal statement on significant leadership contributions to community service, and submit a recommendation from the high school's principal. Website: https://spirit.prudential.com/

Ronald McDonald Charity House Scholarships
The RMHC, offer scholarships to students who have demonstrated academic achievement, leadership and community involvement. The average award is $2,000
Website: http://www.rmhc.org/rmhc-us-scholarships

Samuel Huntington Public Service Award
Established by the energy company National Grid, the Samuel Huntington Public Service Award is granted annually to graduating college seniors who wish to undertake one year of community service anywhere in the world before proceeding on to graduate school or a

professional career. In order to qualify for the $15,000 stipend award, candidates graduating from a U.S. accredited institution must submit a one-page cover letter, service proposal, budget plan, official college transcript, resume, and three letters of recommendation.
Website: https://www9.nationalgridus.com/huntington.asp

Sophia Gokey Scholarship Fund
In loving memory of American Idol alum Danny Gokey's wife who devoted her short lifetime in touching the lives of children, the Sophia L. Gokey Scholarship Fund is designed to help youth achieve their higher education dreams despite significant roadblocks or setbacks from economic status. Eligible high school seniors for the $1,000 award must demonstrate accomplishments in community service and have a cumulative high school GPA of 2.7 or higher.
Website: http://sophiasheart.org/volunteer/

State Farm Good Neighbor Scholarship
The State Farm Companies Foundation believes all children deserve an education that helps them

reach their potential and prepares them for life. The State Farm Good Neighbor Scholarship Program was established to provide financial assistance to fifty high school seniors who plan to attend college, technical, or vocational school, but may not be able to meet the expenses of a higher education without such aid and often do not qualify for other scholarships. These scholarships are for high school seniors with a GPA between 2.5 and 3.2 and who are leaders and volunteers in their communities. There are fifty awards. The average award is for $2,500. For more information, please visit scholarshipamerica.org

Website: https://www.statefarm.com/about-us/community/education-programs/grants-scholarships/foundations-scholarships

Stephen J. Brady Stop Hunger Scholarships
Designed to recognize students who have made a significant impact on the national fight against hunger in America, the Stephen J. Brady STOP Hunger Scholarships are offered by the Sodexo Foundation to students between the ages of 5 and 25 who have demonstrated an on-going commitment to their community by performing

unpaid volunteer work eliminating hunger.
Recipients will receive a $5,000 scholarship for
their education and a matching grant in their
name for the hunger-related charity of their
choosing.
Website: http://us.stop-
hunger.org/home/grants/2016-scholars.html

The Jesse Brown Memorial Youth Scholarship
Program
The Jesse Brown Memorial Youth Scholarship
Program honors young volunteers who are
dedicated to serving veterans. Each year, one
outstanding applicant receives the top
scholarship in the amount of $20,000 to help
fund their higher education. In addition, the top
winner and parent receives an expense paid trip
to DAV National Convention to receive the award
and be recognized for their dedication and
commitment to veterans. Additional scholarships
are awarded in the amounts of $15,000, $10,000,
$7,500 & $5,000.
Website: http://www.dav.org/help-
dav/volunteer/jesse-brown-scholarship/

Tylenol Future Cares Scholars Program

This award is for college students studying healthcare, who have high GPAs and can show community involvement. There are up to 20 awards of $500 - $2,500; ten awards of $10,000; and 30 awards of $5,000.
Website:
https://www.tylenol.com/news/scholarship

Violet Richardson Award
Named after the president of the first Soroptimist club, the Violent Richard Award is granted annually for $2,500 to honor young women who are making a difference in the world through participation in volunteer work, such as community service to end discrimination, fight poverty, assist women who are victims of domestic violence, or mentoring young girls. Eligible candidates for the award must be between the ages of 14 and 17 years old with a firm commitment to improving the lives of women and girls worldwide.
Website:
http://www.soroptimist.org/members/program/ programdocs/violetrichardsonaward/english/vra clubinstructions.pdf

Young Women In Public Affairs
Women aged 16 - 19 who are pursuing careers in government, public policy, and community organizations, and who are involved in community service, should apply for this scholarship. Ten international scholarships of $4,000 and up to 32 scholarships of $1,000 are awarded each year.
Website: http://www.zonta.org/Global-Impact/Education/Young-Women-in-Public-Affairs-Award

SCHOLARSHIPS FOR MINORITY STUDENTS

ABA Diversity Scholarship: $2,500
The Diversity Scholarship focuses on broadening
the number of traditionally underrepresented
groups in the management and operation ranks
of the transportation, travel, and tourism
industry. http://www.buses.org/aba-
foundation/scholarships

ACHE Albert W. Dent Graduate Student
Scholarship: Up to $5,000
The Foundation of the American College of
Healthcare Executives established this
scholarship in honor of Albert W. Dent, the first
African-American Fellow of ACHE. This
scholarship is offered to provide financial aid to
minority students in healthcare management
graduate programs to help offset tuition costs,
student loans and expenses. Offered annually,
the Albert W. Dent Graduate Student Scholarship
is designated for minority students enrolled in
their final year of a healthcare management
graduate program.
www.ache.org/Faculty_Students/dent_scholarshi
p

Actuarial Diversity Scholarship: $4,000
The Actuarial Diversity Scholarship promotes diversity within the profession through an annual scholarship program for Black/African American, Hispanic, Native North American and Pacific Islander students.
http://www.actuarialfoundation.org

Brown and Caldwell Minority Scholarship Program: $5,000
Brown and Caldwell supports organizations like the Society of Women Engineers, National Society of Black Engineers and the Society for Hispanic Professional Engineers. The company has set up a Minority Scholarship Program to help minority groups succeed in the environmental engineering industry.

Coca-Cola Pay It Forward Scholarship Program: $5,000
The Coca-Cola Pay It Forward program returns with a stronger focus on African American moms and their impact on the academic success of their teens. Building on the initiative's accomplishments, this year's program will offer

up to 20 winners each a $5,000 scholarship and an invitation to the all-new Coca-Cola Pay It Forward Academy.

Dr. Wynetta A. Frazier "Sister to Sister" Scholarship: $500
The National Hook-up of Black Women, Inc. was conceived by fourteen (14) spirited women who recognized a need to establish a communications network between women's organizations and individuals to support the Congressional Black Caucus legislative efforts, and to provide a national forum to articulate the needs and concerns of African American.

Herman J. Neal Scholarship: $4,000
This scholarship fund supports African-American students in their pursuit of an accounting education and the CPA designation. The Herman J. Neal scholarship fund provides scholarships to African-American accounting students who show significant potential to become CPAs and demonstrate achievement as well as financial need. These scholarships support students with their junior or senior year, or with the additional

year, (30 semester hours) needed to sit for the CPA Exam which can include graduate studies.

Jesse L. Jackson Sr. Fellows Toyota Scholarship: $25,000

Toyota is partnering with Rainbow PUSH Excel to provide $75,000 scholarships to 10 deserving engineering and business college students through the Jesse L. Jackson Sr. Fellows Scholarships. In addition to the scholarships, Toyota is offering these students the opportunity to work at one of their facilities across North America to gain valuable real-world experience, as well as be paired with mentors from Toyota management to help guide them through the next three years of college.

Mae & Mary Scholarship Fund: Varies

The Mae & Mary Scholarship Fund's mission is to financially assist and to empower young people to experience their unlimited potential through education. Mae & Mary a charitable educational organization dedicated to the advancement of African Americans pursuing careers in medical and health care related fields.

NSHSS STEM Scholarships: $1,000
The NSHSS Foundation provides STEM scholarships for underrepresented groups in order to help reduce financial barriers for those with academic and leadership potential and the desire to pursue STEM careers. We recognize that in order to increase diversity in the technology workforce, we must increase diversity in undergraduates.

Ron Brown Scholarships
http://www.ronbrown.org/

United Negro College Fund Scholarships
http://www.uncf.org/scholarships/uncfscholarship.asp

Jackie Robinson Foundation Scholarships
http://www.jackierobinson.org/

Intel Science Talent Search
http://www.sciserv.org/sts

Thurgood Marshall Scholarship Fund
http://www.thurgoodmarshallfund.org/

United Negro College Fund
http://www.uncf.org/

Broke Scholars Scholarships
http://scholarships.brokescholar.com/

National Society of Black Engineers Scholarships
http://www.nsbe.org/programs/

Black Excel Scholarship Gateways
http://www.blackexcel.org/

LULAC - National Scholastic Achievement Awards
http://mach25.collegenet.com/cgi-
bin/M25/GetScholar?page=10177

Scholarship & Financial Aid Help
http://www.blackexcel.org/fin-sch.html

NAACP Scholarships
http://www.naacp.org/departments/education/s
cholarship_index.html

Black Alliance for Educational Options
Scholarships
http://www.baeo.org/options/privatelyfinanced.j

sp

Historically Black College & University
Scholarships
http://www.iesabroad.org/info/hbcu.html

Hope Scholarships and Lifetime Learning Credits
http://www.ed.gov/offices/OPE/PPI/HOPE/inde
x.html

Presidential Freedom Scholarships
http://www.nationalservice.org/scholarships

Black Student Fund
http://www.blackstudentfund.org/programs/Fin
Aid/financial aidhtml

Chela Education Financing "Gateway to Success
Scholarship"
http://www.loans4students.org/

Congressional Hispanic Scholarships
http://www.chciyouth.org/

Nursing Scholarships
http://www.blackexcel.org/nursing-
scholarships.html

48) College-Bound High School Seniors - Scholarships
http://scholarships.fatomei.com/scholar13.html

AFROTC High School Scholarships
http://www.afrotc.com/

Minority Scholarships
http://www.free-4u.com/minority.html

Scholarships for Minority Accounting Students
http://wwwaicpa.org/members/div/career/mini/smas.html

African American Scholarships
http://www.littleafricacom/scholarship/

Research for Women & Minorities Underrepresented in the Sciences
http://www.research.att.com/academic/urp.htm lhttp://www.research.att.com/academic/urp.html

Tylenol Scholarships
http://scholarship.tylenol.com/

Undergraduate Scholarships (Health)
http://ugsp.info.nih.gov/InfoUGSP.html

STATE FARM INSURANCE Hispanic Scholarships
http://www.statefarm.com/foundati/hispanic.html

National Scholarships at All Levels
http://scholarships.fatomei.com/

Burger King Scholars (Annual Awards)
http://www.bk.com/CompanyInfo/community/B
Kscholars/index.aspx

Ambassadorial Scholarships
http://www.rotary.org/foundation/educational/a
mb_scho/

Baptist Scholarships
http://www.free-
4u.com/baptist_scholarships.html

Methodist Scholarships
http://www.free-
4u.com/methodist_scholarships.html

100 Minority Scholarship Gateways
http://www.blackexcel.org/100minority.html

Hispanic Scholarship Fund
http://www.hsf.net/

Scholarship Research Center: US NEWS
http://12.47.197.196/usnews/

Pacific Northwest Scholarship Guide Online
http://fp2.adhost.com/collegeplan/scholarship/
default.asp

Scholarships For Hispanics
http://www.scholarshipsforhispanics.org/

Actuary Scholarships for Minority Students
http://www.beanactuary.org/minority/

Indian Health Service Scholarships
http://www.ihs.gov/JobsCareerDevelop/DHPS/S
P/spTOC.asp

Minority Undergraduate Fellows Program
http://www.naspa.org/resources/mufp/

Third Wave Foundation Scholarships
http://www.thirdwavefoundation.org/programs/
scholarships.html

Indian Students
http://www.gurgaonscoop.com/story/2005/3/1
4/195141/137

National Association of Black Journalists
Scholarships (NABJ)
http://www.bell-labs.com/fellowships/

The Roothbert Fund Scholarships
http://www.roothbertfund.org/scholarships.php

International Students Help and Scholarships
http://www.iefa.org/

NACME Scholarship Program
http://www.nacme.org/scholarships/

Alpha Kappa Alpha Scholarships
http://www.akaeaf.org/scholarships.html

Martin Luther King Scholarships
http://www.sanantonio.gov/mlk/?res=1024&ver
=true

Chicana/Latina Foundation
http://www.chicanalatina.org/scholarship.html

Congressional Hispanic Caucus Institute
http://www.chci.org/

Morris K. Udall Foundation Scholarships
http://www.udall.gov/p_scholarship.asp

A Better Chance Scholarships
http://www.abetterchance.org/ReferralOrgs&Res
ources/res-coll_native_schol1.html

Asian American Journalist Association
http://www.aaja.org/

American Association of University Women
http://www.aauw.org/fga/fellowships_grants/in
dex.cfm

Alger Association Scholarships
http://www.horatioalgerorg/scholarships

National Security Scholarships Programs
http://www.iie.org/programs/nsep/nsephome.ht
ml

Institutes of Health Scholarship Programs
http://www.iie.org/programs/nsep/nsephome.ht
ml

Adventures in Education
http://adventuresineducation.org/

Union Plus Scholarship Database
http://www.aflcio.org/familyfunresources/colleg
ecosts/scholarcfm

Verizon Scholarship Program
http://foundation.verizon.com/06011.shtml

Cola-Coca Art & Film Scholarships
http://www.youthdevelopment.coca-
cola.com/art_refreshing.html

Red Cross Presidential Intern Program
http://www.redcross.org/images/pdfs/PIP_Fact_
Sheet.pdf

Congressional Black Caucus Scholarships
http://www.cbcfinc.org/Leadership%20Educatio
n/Scholarships/index.html

Microsoft Scholarships
http://www.microsoft.com/college/ss_overview.
mspx

APS Minorities Scholarship Program (Physics)
http://www.aps.org/educ/com/index.html

The Minority/Disadvantaged Scholarship
Program (architecture)
http://www.archfoundation.org/

Engineering Awards and Scholarships
http://www.ieeorg/EduCareers/Awards/UG/ind
ex.cfm

Undergraduate Awards for Women
http://www.biochem.northwestern.edu/resfunds
/undergrad.women.pdf

Undesignated Scholarships (Engineering)
http://students.sae.org/awdscholar/scholarship
s/undesignated/

Scholarships for Minority Accounting Students
http://wwwaicpa.org/members/div/career/mini
/smas.html

Actuarial Scholarships for Minority Students
http://www.beanactuary.org/minority/scholarsh
ip.cfm

Minority Scholarships (All levels)
http://scholarships.fatomei.com/scholar3.html

Findaid: Minority Scholarships
http://www.finaid.org/otheraid/minority.phtml
Native American & Other Scholarships
http://www.abetterchance.org/ReferralOrgs&Res
ources/res-coll_native_schol1.html

Students of Color Scholarships
http://www.financialaid4you.com/index.php/sc
holarships

USA Access Education Scholarships
http://www.usafunds.org/planning/access_to_e
ducation_scholarship/index.html

Fellowships and Scholarships
http://www.sacnas.org/fellow.html

Dow Jones Scholarship and Program Listings
http://djnewspaperfund.dowjones.com/fund/cg
js_min_scholarships.asp

Ernest Hemingway Awards Scholarships
http://djnewspaperfund.dowjones.com/fund/cg
gen_scholarships.asp

Minority Journalism Internships
http://djnewspaperfund.dowjones.com/fund/cg
min_internships.asp

SCHOLARSHIPS FOR VISUAL ARTS

Project Yellow Light Design Contest Scholarship
Available to: College Freshmen through College
Seniors
Award Amount: $2,000
The Project Yellow Light Design Contest
Scholarship is available to high school juniors
and seniors and full – time undergraduate
students. To be considered, you must design a
billboard advertisement that discourages
distracted driving.

NPG 2017 Photography Scholarship Contest
Available to: High School Seniors through College
Juniors
Award Amount: $1,500
The NPG 2017 Photography Scholarship Contest
is open to high school seniors and college
freshmen, sophomores and juniors. You must
submit an original photo with a 40 to 50 word
description, which shows how the environment of
the U.S. is being damaged by population growth.
You must also be a U.S. citizen to qualify for this
award.

Create-a-Greeting Card Scholarship
Available to: High School Freshmen through
Graduate Students, Year 5
Award Amount: $10,000
The Create-A-Greeting Card Scholarship Contest
is open to currently enrolled high school and
college students in the United States. To enter,
you must design a holiday, get well, or birthday
greeting card and submit your work to be judged.
Your photo, art, or graphics submitted must be
your own original work and you must be at least
14 years of age to be eligible for this award.

Milton Fisher Scholarship for Innovation and
Creativity
Deadline: 4/30/17
Available to: High School Juniors through College
Freshmen
Award Amount: $5,000
The Milton Fisher Scholarship for Innovation and
Creativity is available to high school juniors and
seniors, and entering and current college
freshmen. You must be a resident of, or be
planning to attend school in Connecticut or the
New York City metropolitan area. To be eligible,
you must demonstrate how you have solved

artistic, scientific, or technical problems in new or unusual ways; how you have come up with distinctive solutions to problems faced by your school, community, or family; or how you have developed an innovative way to save the environment or improve people's health.

Ula Baker Seecha Scholarship
Available to: College Freshmen through College Seniors
Award Amount: $2,800
The Ula Baker Seecha Scholarship is available to graduates of Kamehameha Schools who are pursuing a career as an artist.
Preference will be given to students focused on the visual arts such as drawing, watercolor painting, and graphic design.

Visual Arts Endowment Scholarship
Available to: College Sophomores through College Seniors
Award Amount: $4,000
The Visual Arts Endowment Scholarship is available to continuing full-time students at the University of California, San Diego majoring in visual arts. This award is based on merit.

Talent Grant – Western Illinois University
Available to: College Freshmen through College Seniors
Award Amount: $400
The Talent Grant is open to art majors at Western Illinois University.

Dutchess Heritage Quilters Scholarship
Available to: College Freshmen through College Sophomores
Award Amount: $1,200
The Dutchess Heritage Quilters Scholarship is available to full-time non-traditional students at Dutchess Community College.
You must be enrolled in either the performing or visual arts programs or the communications program to qualify for this award.

Art Scholarship – Oklahoma City University
Available To: College Freshmen through College Seniors
Award Amount: Varies
The Art Scholarship is available to students at Oklahoma City University.

You must demonstrate talent in art (studio, graphic or photography) to be eligible for this renewable award.

Your selection is based on a portfolio assessment.

Baton Rouge Art League Award
Available to: College Juniors through Graduate Students, Year 5
Award Amount: $250
The Baton Rouge Art League Award is available to junior, senior and graduate students at Louisiana State University.
You must be majoring in art and have a minimum 3.0 GPA to be eligible for this award.

Charles Craig International Travel Award Scholarship
Available to: College Freshmen through College Seniors
Award Amount: $5,000
The Charles Craig International Travel Award Scholarship is available to students at Louisiana State University.
You must be majoring in art to be eligible for this award.

National Gallery of Art Conservation Fellowship
Deadline: Varies
Available to: Graduate School, Year 1 through Year 5
The National Gallery of Art Conservation Fellowship is open to art conservation graduate students with no more than five years of work experience.
You must be interested in the examination and treatment of works of art.
Fellows will focus on two aspects: treatment of the collection and research that culminates in a published paper.
This is a three-year fellowship.

Art Competition – College of Notre Dame of Maryland
Available to: College Freshmen
Award Amount: $3,000
The Art Competition is open to incoming first year and transfer students at the College of Notre Dame of Maryland. Students with artistic talents may submit a portfolio to be eligible for this award.

Robie Robison Visual Arts Award
Available to: College Freshmen through College
Seniors
Award Amount: Varies
The Robie Robison Visual Arts Award is open to
visual arts students at Idaho State University.
You must be an Idaho high school graduate and
have a minimum 2.5 GPA.
You must also be a U.S. citizen to qualify for this
award.
Get more information on the Robie Robison
Visual Arts Award

FIDM National Scholarship Competition
Deadline: Varies
Available to: High School Seniors through College
Freshmen
Award Amount: 100% of Tuition
The Fashion Institute of Design & Merchandising
(FIDM) Scholarship Competition is open to all U.S
high school seniors and graduates who would
like to attend FIDM.
To be considered, you must submit a project in
one of the following categories: Fashion Executive
of Tomorrow, Interior, Designer of Tomorrow,
Graphic Designer of Tomorrow, Fashion Designer

of Tomorrow, Visual Designer of Tomorrow, and Digital Media Artist of Tomorrow.

Projects are judged on creativity, thoughtfulness and promise.

SCHOLARSHIPS FOR THEATER
MAJORS/STUDENTS

Against the Grain Artistic Scholarship
Application Deadlines: May 31, Annually
The Against The Grain Artistic Scholarship
provides financial assistance and promotion of
Asian-American college students pursuing a
major in the performing, visual arts, journalism
and/or mass communications. Scholarship
Winners will be invited to attend our annual
charity event, Fashion for a Passion, held in Fall
in Dallas, Texas. Eligibility:
-Must be of at least 50% Asian and/or Pacific

Application Deadlines: February 01, Annually
The Alys Robinson Stephens Performing Arts
Scholarship was established in 1999 with funds
from the Alumni Society Golf Tournament and
the Alumni Casino Night. The Society supported
the establishment of this scholarship in order to
assist with the recruitment of talented performing
student artists to UAB.

CBC Spouses Heineken USA Performing Arts
Scholarship

This award is for full-time students with majors in the performing arts including, but not limited to, drama, music, dance, opera, marching bands, and other musical ensembles.

Eligibility:
-U.S. citizen or permanent U.S. resident
-Currently/planning to be enrolled in the upcoming academic year as a full-time undergraduate student
-Have a minimum 2.5 GPA

CSUB Armand Hammer Fine Arts Scholarship
This scholarship was established to support CSUB students majoring in Fine Arts (e.g., Theatre, Music, Art, etc.).
Award Criteria:
-Enrolled full-time
-Majoring in the Fine Arts
-Upper-division
-Minimum 3.0 GPA
-Be in the top 20% of the Fine Arts discipline
-Exhibit outstanding talent in their field

CSUB Beglin Family Awards
This scholarship was established by Philip J. and

Kelley H. Beglin. Kelley is a lecturer at CSUB. Two scholarships are awarded one for a nursing student and one for a theare-arts student.

CSUB Channing & Kullijian Arts Scholarship
This scholarship was established by Carol Channing and Harry Kullijian to support creative visual and performing arts students and candidates for teacher credentials in art education. Applicants must be an undergraduate, graduate or credential student enrolled full-time; be pursuing a degree in visual or performing arts or a teaching credential in art education.

Francis D. Lyon Scholarship
The Francis D. Lyon Scholarships are available to students of film making. Mr. Lyon had a distinguished motion picture and television career as a film editor, director and producer. He received an Oscar from the Academy of Motion Picture Arts and Sciences for best film editor in 1948 for the movie "Body and Soul."

Gordon Hay Scholarship
The $5,000 Gordon Hay Scholarship is a merit-based award for an extraordinary graduating

high school senior who is planning to pursue a non-performing career within the performing arts field and demonstrates a personal drive for excellence, scholarly accomplishment, and community engagement.

GRCF Arts Council of Greater Grand Rapids Minority Scholarship
The Arts Council of Greater Grand Rapids Minority Scholarship is open to students of color (African-American, Asian, Hispanic, Native American, Pacific Islander) attending a non-profit public or private college/university majoring in fine arts, including all visual and performing arts. Applicants must have financial need, be a Kent County resident, and have a minimum 2.5 GPA.

GRCF Grand Rapids Combined Theatre Scholarship
The Grand Rapids Combined Theatre Scholarship Fund was founded in 1985 to award college scholarships to students pursuing study in theatre arts. It is supported by ongoing contributions from individuals in the community, and by annual support from Actor's Theatre,

Community Circle Theatre, Grand Rapids Civic Theatre, Heritage Theatre, and Jewish Theatre.

Henry & Joyce W. Sumid Scholarship
Application Deadlines: April 30, Annually
The Henry and Joyce W. Sumid Scholarship is available to high school seniors and college students interested in studying theatre arts and whose legal residence is within these states: Alaska, Arizona, California, Hawaii, Idaho, New Mexico, Oregon, Utah, and Washington.

Hope College Distinguished Artist Awards - Theatre
Each year at Hope College, up to 60 Distinguished Artist Award (DAA) scholarships are given to students with strong academic records and outstanding creative abilities in art, dance, music, theatre or creative writing. Renewable for four years, the DAA's provide eligible students with $2,500 each year toward their college costs.
ISF offers many joint scholarships to Muslim Student/University Alumni groups that share its common mission and vision. ISF is honored to work with the UC Irvine Muslim Alumni

Association to host the ISF-UCI Muslim Alumni Scholarship to enable UCI students to achieve their goals in higher education.

Indiana State University Jack E. and Virginia Carpenter Fine Arts Scholarship
Established in 1999 by Cheryl and C. Thomas Steiner to honor Cheryl's parents, Jack and Virginia Bradbury. Dr. and Mrs. Bradbury are both alumni of Indiana State University. The scholarship, which was established to assist needy students in the arts, is based in the College of Arts and Sciences.

ISC-IIOC Scholarship
ISF supports Islamic organizations and mosques by planning and managing joint scholarships. ISF is honored to host the ISF-IIOC scholarship of the Islamic Institute of Orange County (IIOC).
Eligibility:
-Active member of the IIOC
-Attending an accredited university in the U.S.
-Majoring in an ISF-supported field of study
-Maintaining a minimum 3.0 GPA

ISF National Scholarships
The Islamic Scholarship Fund (ISF) is a non-
profit 501(c)(3) entity founded in 2009 whose
mission is to address the under-representation of
American Muslims in the fields and occupations
that influence public opinion and make public
policy.

ISF-MCA Scholarship
ISF supports Islamic organizations and mosques
by planning and managing joint scholarships. ISF
is honored to host the ISF-MCA Scholarship of
the Muslim Community Association of the Bay
Area, MCA. The ISF-MCA Scholarship program is
only open to members and individuals affiliated
with the MCA.

ISF-MCC Scholarship
ISF supports Islamic organizations and mosques
by planning and managing joint scholarships. ISF
is honored to host the ISF-MCC Scholarship of
the Muslim Community Center East Bay, MCC.
The ISF-MCC Scholarship program is only open
to members and individuals affiliated with the
MCC.

ISF-MSA West Scholarship
ISF offers many joint scholarships to Muslim
Student/University Alumni groups that share its
common mission and vision. ISF is honored to
work with the MSA-West to host the ISF-MSA
West Scholarship.

Eligibility:
-Be attending an accredited MSA West member
university in the U.S. and attended the MSA West
Conference
-Majoring in an ISF supported field of study

ISF-SRVIC Scholarship
ISF offers many joint and sponsored scholarships
with partner organizations, masjids,
student/alumni associations and private
sponsors that share its mission and vision. SF
supports Islamic organizations and mosques by
planning and managing joint scholarships.

JSU Alabama Drama Scholarships
Each year, the JSU drama department awards
thousands of dollars in scholarships to talented,
hard-working drama students. Scholarships are
awarded through an application process that

includes auditions or interviews. Students must also demonstrate a commitment to JSU productions and high academic standards.

Kevin Spacey Foundation Scholarship
The Kevin Spacey Foundation works in partnership with universities in the UK and the US to offer KSF Scholarships to talented applicants of performing arts and film undergraduate programs.

Seven (7) one-year KSF Scholarships covering $10,000 of the tuition fees are available across the following programs:
-BFA Acting
-BFA Acting for Film, TV, Voice-over and Commercials

Lee A. Lyman Memorial Music Scholarship
The Lee A. Lyman Memorial Music Scholarship was established by VSAC in 1995 in memory of Lee A. Lyman. Lee was active in the Vermont financial aid community for more than 20 years and was director of VSAC's Education Loan Finance Program for 10 years (1984–1994).

Lycoming College Theater Scholarships
Students planning to pursue a major or a minor
in theatre are encouraged to audition with faculty
from the Theatre Department.

Robert W. Thunen Memorial Scholarship
Applications for the Thunen Memorial
Scholarship may be submitted by full-time
students who desire to study illumination as a
career. Applications for the Thunen Memorial
Scholarship may be made by those who will be an
undergraduate junior, senior or graduate student
(fall semester only) in an accredited four-year
college or university located in Northern
California, Nevada, Oregon or Washington.

Sophie and Hans Scholl Memorial Scholarship
This scholarship is open to all Nevada public high
school seniors. The scholarship is for students
wishing to study German OR a German related
field. For instance, if a student majors in
international diplomacy, and he/she is required
to take a foreign language, then that student
would qualify provided he/she chooses a German
course.

Eligibility:
-Nevada high school seniors who either plan

Sue Dilts Memorial Art Scholarship
The Gratiot County Community Foundation, incorporated in 1992, is a vehicle for receiving charitable gifts that will remain forever in Gratiot County. As a non-profit corporation, we are classified as a public charity under the Internal Revenue Code, making donors eligible for federal tax deductions and a State of Michigan tax credit. Gifts to the Foundation may be in cash, and real estate.

The Fulbright Program
The Fulbright Program operates in more than 155 countries worldwide and has provided approximately 310,000 participants with the opportunity to study, teach, or conduct research in each others' countries and exchange ideas. Approximately 8,000 prestigious, competitive, merit-based grants are awarded annually in most academic disciplines and fields of study.

The Jay Franke Scholarship
The mission of Diabetes Scholars Foundation is

to support activities related to education for and about children with diabetes. This includes but is not limited to funding scholarships for diabetes education conferences and higher education.

The Jewish Federation of Metropolitan Chicago Academic Scholarship
Educational scholarship funds from grants administered by the Jewish Federation of Metropolitan Chicago are available for Jewish college and graduate students. Approximately $500,000 is available each year for full-time students, predominantly those legally domiciled in the metropolitan Chicago area, who are identified as having promise for significant contributions in their chosen careers.

The Marco Island Foundation for the Arts Scholarship
The Marco Island Foundation for the Arts (MIFA) awards scholarships to deserving students who reside on Marco Island, FL. and who have demonstrated excellence in visual, literary or performing arts, and intend to study one of the arts at the college level. Scholarships to be

awarded will be up to $1,000.

The Virginia Budge Award for the Creative and
Performing Arts
The Virginia Budge Award exists to create,
promote, develop, sponsor, sustain, facilitate and
further the arts within Butler County, Ohio. For
the mission of the committee, the term "arts"
shall be defined and literally construed to include
the making or doing of things that have form and
beauty, and to encompass all forms of arts
including the arts of music, painting, sculpture,
and dance, theatre.

Vectorworks Design Scholarship
The program supports promising students on two
levels. First, Vectorworks Design Scholarships
will be presented to multiple winners around the
globe. Prize packages include $3,000,
Vectorworks Designer with Renderworks software
for a computer lab at the winner's school and
virtual or in-person training for faculty and
students.

Walt Disney Imaginations Design Competition Project Challenge

Imaginations is a design competition created and sponsored by Walt Disney Imagineering with the purpose of seeking out and nurturing the next generation of diverse Imagineers. Started in 1991 by Disney Legend and Imagineering executive Marty Sklar, the program has grown to include a separate version sponsored by Hong Kong Disneyland.

SCHOLARSHIPS FOR DANCE MAJORS

Arts for Life! Scholarship
Arts for Life! annually awards $2,000
scholarships to 25 graduating high school seniors
in Florida who demonstrate excellence in creative
writing, dance, drama, music or visual art. In
addition to the $2,000 cash award, the Arts for
Life! College Matching Program provides an
additional matching in-kind scholarship, worth a
minimum of $1,000, to award winners attending
one of these.

Ashley E. Ketcher Memorial Scholarship
The purpose of the Ashley E. Ketcher Memorial
Scholarship is to provide educational funds to
support an Auburn High School CAPA student
planning to attend an accredited college or
university.

Criteria:
-Applicant must be a graduating Auburn High
School senior in the CAPA program who
-Has an interest and prior experience in the
performing arts

-Has a cumulative GPA of at least 2.5/4.0

Austin College Art Scholarships
Austin College art scholarships are awarded to students with talents in studio art, who may or may not intend a major or minor in art. A limited number of awards are available each year. Recipients are required to maintain satisfactory participation in at least one art or art history course each year that they receive the award and must remain full-time students in good academic standing.

CBC Spouses Heineken USA Performing Arts Scholarship
This award is for full-time students with majors in the performing arts including, but not limited to, drama, music, dance, opera, marching bands, and other musical ensembles.

Eligibility:
-U.S. citizen or permanent U.S. resident
-Currently/planning to be enrolled in the upcoming academic year as a full-time undergraduate student

-Have a minimum 2.5 GPA

DDF/DREAM Dance Performing Arts Scholarship Award

Specifically for college students and high school seniors who are enrolled in a dance and performing arts degree program. The Dream scholarship award is designed to support, improve, and increase opportunities for students who wish to further their dance/performing arts training for a career in dance and the performing arts.

Dr. Edward and Anne Link Fund Scholarship

To be eligible for the Dr. Edward and Anne Link Fund Scholarship, applicants must be a Shelby County resident maintaining a college GPA of not less than 3.0 and are pursuing a major in visual arts, performing arts, or creative writing toward a Bachelor's or a Master's degree. Applicants must have completed at least one year of post-secondary education.

Furman University Art Scholarships

Art Department Scholarships are available for incoming students who wish to actively participate in the Art Department either as majors or non-majors. We have a number of competitive scholarships that can be combined with any academic merit-based scholarships students receive on the basis of their application for admission.

HEEF Arts Scholarship Program
Students must enroll in a four-year college and major in: art, dance, drama, music, performance art, video, visual arts, new media or related major. May be renewable based on available funding.

Eligibility:
-Latino/a who has lived in Orange County (OC), CA for the past six (6) years

Hope College Distinguished Artist Awards - Dance
Each year at Hope College up to 60 Distinguished Artist Award (DAA) scholarships are given to students with strong academic records and outstanding creative abilities in art, dance, music, theatre, or creative writing. Renewable for four years, the DAA's provide eligible students

with $2,500 each year toward their college costs.
DAA recipients also take part in a variety of
opportunities set up

Iowa Scholarships for the Arts
At the time of application, student applicants
must be enrolled at the senior class level in an
Iowa high school and display proven artistic
ability in the areas of music, dance, visual arts,
theater or literature. Scholarship funds are
awarded contingent upon recipients being
accepted as full-time undergraduate students at
a fully-accredited Iowa college or university.

JSU Alabama Drama Scholarships
Each year, the JSU drama department awards
thousands of dollars in scholarships to talented,
hard-working drama students. Scholarships are
awarded through an application process that
includes auditions or interviews. Students must
also demonstrate a commitment to JSU
productions and high academic standards.

MSU Moorhead Incoming Freshman Talent Scholarships
MSUM Talent Scholarships are awarded to Minnesota State University Moorhead students who demonstrate exceptional talent in the areas of art, music, cinema arts and digital technologies or theater arts. Department faculty select talent awards. Contact the departments directly for more information and application procedures.

Tupelo Elvis Fan Club Scholarship
Eligibility:
-You must be a resident of Mississippi and enrolled as a senior at a Mississippi high school
-You must sing, dance or play a musical instrument and submit a performance MP4 video for review by the selection committee. If chosen as a semi-finalist, you will be invited to perform live at the Finale to be held in Tupelo, Mississippi on a date to be announced later.

SCHOLARSHIPS FOR SCIENCE, TECHNOLOGY, ENGINEERING AND MATH (STEM)

NSHSS Foundation STEM Scholarship
Available to: High School Seniors through College Freshmen
Award Amount: $1,000
The NSHSS Foundation STEM Scholarship is available to graduating high school seniors. You must plan to enter a college to study in a science, technology, engineering, or mathematics field. You must have at least a 3.0 GPA to be eligible for this award.

Asia SiVon Cottom Scholarship
Available to: College Freshmen through Graduate Students, Year 5
Award Amount: Awards from $500 to $2,000
The Asia SiVon Cottom Scholarship is available to high school seniors, undergraduate, and graduate students. You must be pursuing a degree in science, technology, engineering, or math to be eligible for this award. You must also submit a minimum 300 – word essay on the effects and aftermath of September 11th on

today's society, what you plan to achieve through college that can possibly impact the community and / or the world, and why you should receive a Memorial Scholarship.

Anne Maureen Whitney Barrow Memorial Scholarship
Available to: College Freshmen through College Seniors
Award Amount: $7,000
The Anne Maureen Whitney Barrow Memorial Scholarship is open to full-time female students majoring in engineering.

Youth Activity Grant – Explorers Club
Award: $5,000
Available to: College Freshmen through College Seniors
The Youth Activity Grant is available to full-time high school seniors and undergraduate college students to enable them to participate in field research in the natural sciences under the supervision of a qualified scientist and/or institution.
In addition to the application, you must submit a three-page explanation of your proposed project

in your own words and two letters of recommendation to be eligible for this award.

Astronaut Scholarship in Science and Technology
Available to: College Sophomores through Graduate Students, Year 5
Award Amount: 18 Awards of $10,000
The Astronaut Scholarship in Science and Technology is open to students majoring in engineering, natural science, applied science, or mathematics.
You must attend one of the participating educational institutions to be considered for this award. U.S. citizenship is also a requirement.

Royce Osborne Minority Student Scholarship
Available to: College Freshmen through College Seniors
Award Amount: 5 Awards of $4,000
Sponsored by the American Society of Radiologic Technologists, the Royce Osborne Minority Student Scholarship is open to minority students who are attending an entry-level radiologic sciences program.
You must have a minimum 3.0 GPA, demonstrate financial aid, and be a United States citizen or

permanent resident to be considered for this award.

Siemens Clinical Advancement Scholarship Program
Available to: College Freshmen through Graduate Students, Year 5
Award Amount: 4 Awards of $5,000
Sponsored by the American Society of Radiologic Technologists, the Siemens Clinical Advancement Scholarship Program is open to undergraduate and graduate students who are pursuing a baccalaureate or graduate degree in the radiologic sciences or health sciences.

URSA Scholarship Program
Available to: College Juniors through College Seniors
Award Amount: $1,000
The University Space Research Association Scholarship to full-time students who have shown a career interest in the physical sciences or engineering with an emphasis on space research or space science education.
This includes, but is not limited to, aerospace engineering, astronomy, bio-physics, chemistry,

chemical engineering, computer science,
electrical engineering, geophysics, geology,
mathematics, mechanical engineering, science
education and physics.
In order to apply, you must have completed at
least two (2) years of college credits by the time
the award is received.
U.S. citizenship is required as well as a minimum
cumulative GPA of 3.50.

Ventures Scholars Program
Award: $10,000
Available to: High School Freshmen through
College Freshmen
The Ventures Scholars Program is open to
underrepresented and first-generation college-
bound students. You must be pursuing a math-
or science-based career to be considered for this
award.

Women in Wireless Communications Scholarship
Available to: College Freshmen through College
Sophomores
Award Amount: Varies

The Women in Wireless Communications Scholarship is available to female students in the College of Technology at Idaho State University. You must be enrolled in the electronic wireless telecommunications program and demonstrate a strong academic performance, involvement in co-curricular activities and future goals in the field of wireless communications to be eligible for this award.

NASA Internships
Available to: Minimum Age 16 Years
Provided by National Aeronautics and Space Administration (NASA), the NASA Internships are available to high school through graduate level students attending full-time accredited programs appropriate to the NASA internship. You must be a U.S. citizen, majoring in wide-variety of majors ranging from business to science and engineering to be considered for this internship.
College-level interns must maintain a minimum GPA of 3.0. As an intern, you will engage in scientific or engineering research, development, and operations activities.
In addition, there are non-technical internship opportunities to engage in professional activities

which support NASA business and administrative processes.

Rugh Family Scholarship
Available to: College Freshmen through College Seniors
Award Amount: Varies
The Rugh Family Scholarship is open to students at the Virginia Military Institute.
You must demonstrate capability in engineering or the physical sciences to qualify for this award.

Rugh Family Scholarship
Available to: College Freshmen through College Seniors
Award Amount: Varies
The American Society of Heating, Refrigerating and Air-Conditioning Engineers Undergraduate Engineering Scholarship is available to undergraduate students who are enrolled in an ABET-accredited program leading to a Bachelor of Science or a Bachelor of Engineering Science degree.
Your course of study must be related to heating, ventilation, air conditioning and refrigeration. A minimum 3.0 GPA is required.

Chevron Society of Women Engineers Scholarship
Available to: College Sophomores through College
Juniors
Award Amount: Varies
The Chevron Society of Women Engineers
Scholarship is available to sophomores and
juniors at the University of Idaho. You must have
a minimum GPA of 3.0, be a member of the UI
Soceity of Women Engineers, and be majoring in
one of the following fields to be eligible for this
award: civil engineering, chemical engineering,
electrical engineering, mechanical engineering
and computer science.

Dr. William W.L. "Bill" Taylor Memorial
Scholarship Competition
Available to: College Freshmen through College
Seniors
Award Amount: Varies
The Dr. William W.L. "Bill" Taylor Memorial
Scholarship Competition is available to students
attending or planning to attend a Washington DC
Metropolitan-area university or college.
You must also be a U.S. citizen and demonstrate
academic achievement through your GPA. You
must be registered for full-time study as a

student in good standing in your high school, college or university.

In addition, you must demonstrate your participation in a Very Low Frequency (VLF) research project, leadership abilities, and your motivation as a physical science student to be eligible for this award.

University Space Research Deadline: Varies
Available to: College Juniors

The University Space Research Association Scholarship to full-time students who have shown a career interest in the physical sciences or engineering with an emphasis on space research or space science education.

This includes, but is not limited to, aerospace engineering, astronomy, bio-physics, chemistry, chemical engineering, computer science, electrical engineering, geophysics, geology, mathematics, mechanical engineering, science education and physics.

In order to apply, you must have completed at least two (2) years of college credits by the time the award is received. U.S. citizenship is required as well as a minimum cumulative GPA of 3.50.

SCHOLARSHIPS IN SCIENCE, TECHNOLOGY, ENGINEERING, MATH (STEM) FOR WOMEN

BHW Women in STEM Academic Scholarship
Deadline: April 1. Award: $3,000 and another
scholarship opens this month. Website:
https://thebhwgroup.com/scholarship
Society of Women Engineers Scholarships
Deadline: Incoming freshman May 1 and
Sophomore through graduate school February
15. Awards: Scholarships range from $1,000 to
$15,000 each and some are renewable, Website:
http://societyofwomenengineers.swe.org/index.p
hp/swe-scholarships

American Association of University Women
Deadlines: Vary (check website for your state).
Awards: $500 to $10,000 depending on your
state. Website: http://www.aauw.org/what-we-
do/educational-funding-and-awards/local-
scholarships/

National Center for Women & IT Collegiate Award
Awards vary and include exclusive access to
scholarships, internships, and job opportunities.
Eligibility: College females with a major or minor

in computing, has qualifying GPA and attends an NCWIT Academic Alliance institution. Website: https://www.aspirations.org/participate/college-students

American Chemical Society Scholars Program Deadline: March 1. Eligibility: African American, Hispanic, or American Indian high school seniors or college freshman, sophomores, or juniors pursuing a college degree in the chemical sciences or chemical technology. *Note: Not just for women* Awards: Up to $5,000 Website: https://www.acs.org/content/acs/en/funding-and-awards/scholarships/acsscholars.html

Engineergirl Scholarships Deadline: February 1. Eligibility: 3rd to 12th grade female students. Awards: $100 to $500. Website: http://www.engineergirl.org/32376.aspx

National Center for Women & IT Deadline is typically in November. Awards vary. Eligibility: Girls age 13 and up and still in high school. Website:

https://www.aspirations.org/participate/high-school

Angela Award Deadline: Typically December annually. Eligibility: Female student in grades 5–8 who is a resident of the United States, US Territories, or Canada, and is enrolled in full time public, private, or home school. Award: $1,000 US EE Savings Bond or Canadian Savings Bond. Website:
http://www.nsta.org/about/awards.aspx
Conrad Challenge Spirit of Innovation Award Deadline: October annually Eligibility: Team event for high school students at 13 to 18. Award: $10,000 in seed money to fund your team project. Website:
http://www.conradchallenge.org/overview-of-program/

Microsoft Hello Cloud Scholarship Deadline: June 1, 2017 Eligibility: 16 years old and up and attend accredited high school Award: $1,000 Website:
https://blogs.msdn.microsoft.com/microsoftimag ine/2016/09/19/coding-for-the-cloud-could-win-you-100/

Association for Women in Mathematics
Deadline: January 31 Eligibility: 6th grade
students through undergraduate. Awards:
Amounts vary for each grade group. Website:
https://sites.google.com/site/awmmath/progra
ms/essay-contest

We want to hear from you! Let us know your successes as you work through this process

http://www.thescholarshipshark.com/contact

Online Courses on College Admissions and College Financing

Want to dig deeper with finding scholarships?
Feeling overwhelmed and frustrated with the admissions process?
Want to know how to write winning scholarship essays?

Enroll in our online courses
http://www.thescholarshipshark.com

✓ Self-paced courses
✓ For individuals and families
✓ Easy to understand
✓ Convenient and flexible
✓ Lifetime access to course

Contact Us

To contact Pam for speaking opportunities, media requests or interviews, please send an email to info@thescholarshipshark.com

Find us online at:
www.TheScholarshipShark.com
Facebook.com /ScholarshipShark
Twitter.com @BiteCollegeDebt
LinkedIn /in/ScholarshipShark

About Pam

Pam Andrews is a College Admissions Coach and Scholarship Strategist. Pam has earned a certificate from Columbia University Teachers College in College Advising. She is the creator of The Scholarship Shark – a book and an e-course to help you find and win scholarships. Pam is a homeschooling mom with children in elementary school to college. In addition to being a homeschool mother who is active in her local support group,

Made in the USA
Lexington, KY
28 September 2019